Things
About
Canada

and 383
Pretty Cool Things
Geordie Telfer

BLUE
BIKE
BOOKS

The Publisher: Blue Bike Books
Website: www.bluebikebooks.com

Library and Archives Canada Cataloguing in Publication

Telfer, Geordie
     1001 (618) awesome: And 383 pretty cool things about Canada. / Geordie Telfer.

ISBN 978-1-926700-42-7

     1. Canada—Miscellanea. 2. Canada—History. 3. Canada—Biography. I. Title. II. Title: One thousand one (618) awesome: And 383 pretty cool things about Canada.

FC60.T42 2013   971   C2013-900630-3

Project Director: Nicholle Carrière
Project Editor: Kathy van Denderen
Cover Image: Gerry Dotto
Illustrations: Pat Bidwell, Roger Garcia, Patrick Hénaff, Graham Johnson, Djorde Todorovic, Peter Tyler, Roly Wood

Produced with the assistance of the Government of Alberta, Alberta Multimedia Development Fund.

We acknowledge the financial support of the Government of Canada through the Canada Book Fund (CBF) for our publishing activities.

 Canadian Heritage   Patrimoine canadien

PC: 1

DEDICATION

For Valin—the most awesome person I know

CONTENTS

FOREWORD

When talking about Canada and its awesome/cool factor, sometimes it seemed as though 1001 items weren't enough to fully celebrate the many, many, many awesome and cool things that characterize this country. It's one of those topics that everyone has an opinion on. Family, friends, my publisher and editors all had suggestions as to what they thought should be in the book. I'm happy to say that I think we were able to fit everything in. No doubt readers will have their own opinions, as well they should. The intent of this book is not to be a comprehensive listing of all that is awesome (or cool) about Canada. Instead, readers should look at it as a conversation starter—what things would *you* include? On a personal note, while writing the book, I started to make an informal bucket list of places and sights in Canada I had not yet seen. It is a long list. And it is full of awesomely cool adventures yet to be had.

–Geordie Telfer

618 AWESOME THINGS

Before it fell so effortlessly from the lips of valley girls and gnarly dudes, the word "awesome" was understood to describe something that inspired feelings of actual awe—something amazing, perhaps slightly unbelievable and possibly a bit scary. Happily, in this case, we've chosen to use the word "awesome" in the sense that valley girls and gnarly dudes use it, which is to say, meaning, more or less, "pretty great." Because, let's face it, while there is much about Canada that is amazing, slightly unbelievable and a bit scary, most of it is pretty great.

DAY-TO-DAY LIVING

Take a walk down any street in Canada (or across the tundra, through the snow or up a mountain pathway), and you're wading through 1001 things that make awesome the fabric of daily life in Canada. They'll make you feel awesomely proud, awesomely embarrassed, awesomely safe and sometimes just profoundly puzzled. If you live in Canada, you may not think twice about what makes day-to-day living awesome in the Great White North. If you're a newcomer to our country, all of these things will be awesomely new to you, for which we Canadians say, "Sorry" and "Thank you" all in the same breath.

Multiculturalism

Widely touted as a good thing in the 1970s and 1980s, multiculturalism has come under fire in recent years. But whether you believe it has been a success or a failure, the practice of encouraging immigration and cultural diversity has shaped Canada in an awesome way. Like it or not, it's who we are, so you might as well just suck it up.

Separation of Church and State

Sane people regard the separation of church and state as a good thing. We firmly believe in your right to practise your faith. We also firmly believe in your right to responsible representation in the political arena—we just don't believe in mixing them. Freedom of faith is doing pretty well these days, but most would argue that political representation in this country is anything but responsible.

Gay Marriage

Not only is it legal in Canada, but it was *already* legal in eight out of the 10 provinces *before* the federal passage of Bill-C38 in 2005. And now that we're done touting this long-overdue awesome thing, it's time to move on and just get used to it as something mundane in its normality (though legal enforcement of basic human rights is always awesome, even when its necessity is sad).

Three- (Plus) Party System

Every 15 or 20 years, one of the major political parties takes a hit, leading to mergers of other parties and doomsayers predicting the imminent demise of either the Liberals, the NDP or the Progressive Conservative party. Oh wait, the PCs *did* collapse, which led to the Reform and Alliance parties merging with the PCs to form the Conservative Party of Canada. Anyway, I have no empirical evidence, but I do think that the three-party system means that Canadians tend to be less oppositional and more open to compromise, always able to see that there's another way.

Bilingualism

You may not be fully bilingual, but you've got to admit that it's awesome to know what a *pamplemousse* is and what *meilleur avant* means and why the word *arrêt* can save your life (though the red octagonal sign should give you a hint). And if you are fully bilingual, then your job prospects are better and your potential for pay is higher. "Good day. Bonjour." Honourable mention goes to *beurre d'arachides* and *jus d'ananas*.

The World Thinks We're Apathetic, But We Just Don't Care

Are we apathetic? Makes no difference to me either way, but on the international stage, this impression lends Canucks a lazy aura of slacker cool, though you'd be hard-pressed to find any Canadians willing to admit they enjoy this reputation. (Maybe we do; maybe we don't. Who cares?)

FACTS OF LIFE

Second Largest Country by Area

We're just over half the size of Russia and barely eke past the U.S. (thanks a lot, Alaska) in terms of area, but still, we're proud to be number two, because the size of our geopolitical package does matter. It's fun to watch the jaws of visitors from the UK, Ireland or Europe hit the floor when they realize that driving across Canada takes five to six days and not a couple of hours.

Lots of Space

Because we're well endowed from a real estate point of view, we have an abundance of room to get away from one another when our politics or hockey teams aren't compatible. This makes us calm, pragmatic and happy to have someone else in our sleeping bag to keep us warm.

Fewer Guns

Statistically speaking, 25 to 30 percent of Canadians own a gun. There are 30 guns for every 100 people. In the U.S., there are just over 88 guns per 100 people. This means that Canadians shoot each other less often. We decline to advance any further argument as to why this is an awesome thing.

SPREADING THE SOCIAL SAFETY NET

Free Health Care

It's awesome. Canada has it. End of discussion. Moving on.

Baby Bonus

And once you've had your baby, as well as reaping the benefits of a civilized, humane parental-leave system, some level of government or another will also throw dribs and drabs of money at you each month.

Year-long Parental Leave

In Canada, new parents can take almost one year off work with their Employment Insurance paying up to half of their regular wage (or 32 weeks in Québec, but with more money). And that's not including any other compensation parents may receive from their employers. South of the border, there is *no* federally mandated parental leave, although some states offer six to twelve *weeks* of parental leave. Can you imagine sending a three-month-old to daycare?

Daycare in Québec

This is a contentious topic. For parents, subsidized daycare in Québec costs about $7 per day or $140 per month. Anywhere else in the country, you're looking at between $900 and upward of $1500 per month. The contentious part is because the Québec system is widely seen as being bankrupt and subsidized, in some ways, by taxpayers outside the province. Still, if you're one of the parents elsewhere in the country paying through the nose for childcare, the Québec model looks not just awesome but awesomely awesome.

Employment Insurance

What used to be Unemployment Insurance (UI) eventually morphed into Employment Insurance (EI). In a bygone golden age, EI was awesomely easy to claim—after all, it was (and is) *your* money, deducted from your paycheque by a benevolent government with your best interests at heart. Now, EI is much harder to claim, with the government thinking up increasingly rigorous ways to keep *your* money in *their* pockets. Just remember, should you be fortunate enough to qualify for EI, you should always fill out your fortnightly assessment as follows: Yes. Yes. Yes. No. Yes. (Or something like that.)

LIFE AT HOME

Milk in Plastic Bags

It's hilarious to watch visiting Americans point and gawk at dairy shelves in grocery stores. Once they've recovered from the sheer shock of the discovery, they will do one of two things: shake their heads in bafflement and disapproval—*Milk! In plastic bags! WTF? It's just not natural!*—or they may simply run away, unable to cope with the idea much less the reality of *milk in plastic bags!* "Jethro, thim thar Canadians have *milk in plastic bags!*"

Kids' TV

Canadians are good at making kids' TV shows. Not everyone would argue that a nation's ability to make laudable children's programming makes it awesome, but I do, and I'm the one writing this book. The CBC and other public broadcasters have blazed a long trail for kid-friendly shows, but young-at-heart independent production companies and private broadcasters have followed suit as well.

Leaders in Web and Social Media Use

Canadians were (and are) fast adopters of both the Internet and of social media (such as Facebook). This doesn't mean that we invented it or that we were the first to jump on the bandwagon. What it does mean is that more of us jumped on the bandwagon faster. That was good for the rest of the world since by the time they got around to Internet dating, all the people already online were awesome Canadians. (This last point isn't factually verifiable, but sometimes there's truth in flippancy.)

DOLLARS AND SENSE

Loonies and Toonies

Our $1 and $2 coins allow all Canadians to release their inner pirates since we can walk into a tavern (which may or may not be in the throes of a swashbuckling brawl by cutthroat ruffians), plonk down a handful of coins and order a pint of grog. When toonies were introduced in 1996, some people went so far as to call them "doubloons," a portmanteau for "double loonie." My argument is that anything that helps a country's citizens to feel more like pirates is necessarily an awesome thing.

Colourful Money (That Melts)

Canada has always been known for having colourful paper currency (much to the bafflement of Americans), and this awesome trait will remain. But now our bills are printed on a sort of plastic that is awesomely strange for those of us used to actual linen-based paper (first we abandoned the gold standard, and now our money is made out of plastic—what next?) And this new "paper" money also melts if it you leave it too close to a heat source.

No More Pennies!

The Canadian Mint has recently announced that pennies are to be discontinued (finally!). Although sad in a way, the public outcry at the abolishment of the penny has been notable for its absence, probably because pennies are completely useless and a nuisance to boot. They are the Brussels sprouts of pocket change. Their eventual eradication will be awesome!

A MISCELLANY OF AWESOMENESS

Courteous Border Guards

Canadian border guards are infamously more polite than their U.S. counterparts. Americans themselves are the first to admit this, sometimes citing suspicious guards who appear reluctant to allow U.S. citizens to *return to their own country*. Canadian border guards, on the other hand, are known for being more nonchalant and *not* addressing all male travellers thusly: "Hey, guy."

Canada Post

Fast becoming redundant (with the advent of email) and ever less reliable, Canada Post is awesome for its unpredictability. A plain old letter sent with regular postage can travel from one end of a large city to the other overnight, and yet a package for which the sender has paid extra (complete with a tracking number) to ensure delivery within two business days can get completely lost with no record of it ever having existed in the first place.

Stores Are Open on Sunday (Finally)

The story of Sunday shopping is different in every province, but in Ontario, it took until *1992* for storeowners to be able to legally open their doors for business on the Sabbath. Thanks in part to the willingness of Toronto furrier Paul Magder to go bankrupt by incurring $500,000 in fines in order to keep his business open on Sunday, stores (in Ontario) can legally be open on Sundays. Seriously? 1992? Well, better late than never.

We Leave Movie Stars Alone (For the Most Part)

Imagine you're somewhere in Canada and you see a movie star walking down the street. What do you do? If you're like most of us, you probably do a double take and then keep walking, intent on getting to wherever it is you're going. Sure, a few bad apples will hector celebrities by clamouring for autographs and quoting lines from their movies back at them, but for the most part, we try to leave the famous folks alone, not wanting to bother them or make them feel uncomfortable. We suspect they like it, but we don't know for sure because we would never presume to ask.

CLOTHING

The garments and accoutrements that follow are not exclusively Canadian so much as they have become associated with the "True North Strong and Free," either in our minds or the minds of others. Or maybe they're just awesome.

Mittens (on Grown-ups)

Kids all over the world wear mittens, but Canada is one of the few places on earth where you'll see adults wearing them, too, be it driving across the tundra on a Ski-doo or walking to work through the city streets. Anyone who has to spend significant amounts of time outdoors (such as film crews, bike couriers and postal workers) quickly learns that gloves don't always cut it, and keeping your fingers toasty together in a pair of mitts is way more awesome (and comfortable, too).

Tuques

These knitted, dome-shaped winter caps often have a small pom-pom on top that does not seem to detract from their awesome Canadianess. Tuques are equally at home atop the heads of rugged lumberjacks, sexy ski bunnies or regular folk out and about their everyday business. It's not as though Canada is the only place you'll see people wearing tuques (far from it), but in our own minds, these friendly looking winter hats are emblematic of a presumed national character.

Parkas

People all over the world wear parkas, and a lot of them live in Canada. Canadians also rightly or wrongly suppose that Americans assume all Canadians wear parkas 365 days a year. It's an awesome example of projecting another nation's cultural assumptions about us back on ourselves so that many Canucks now identify parkas as being specifically Canadian when they're not.

Mukluks

Besides being beautiful examples of ancient and functional Inuit crafts (leather working and beading), these knee-high boots from north of the Arctic Circle are also laudable for their name, which is awesomely satisfying when spoken aloud. *Mukluks.* Go ahead and say it as many times as you want—it doesn't get old.

Snowshoes

Pleasant for recreational jaunts and undoubtedly useful in the snow-swept far north, snowshoes, for anyone who has ever tried to wade through waist-deep snow, are one of the most awesome inventions ever. *What a freaking great idea!* That it's doubtful whether 95 percent of Canadians alive today have ever worn a pair of snowshoes has in no way prevented these variously shaped, webbed, wooden frames from becoming associated with the Great White North and its presumed coating of permanent snow.

Bunny Hug

A hoodie by any other name is still a hoodie, and that's exactly what a bunny hug is. What is awesome about bunny hugs is that they're called bunny hugs (occasionally) by people in Saskatchewan. No one knows why this is, but it is, nonetheless.

Roots

For many, Roots is the quintessential Canadian clothing company, its name echoing wholesomeness and nature, while describing a vaguely preppy line of casual wear. The truly awesome thing about the brand is the stares you get if go to Australia and wear clothing proudly emblazoned with the company's name. That's because Down Under, "roots" is Aussie slang for what hipster Brits would call "shagging." If your name is Randy, you should probably just stay home.

Anoraks

The forerunner of the hoodie (or bunny hug, depending on what part of Canada you live in), anoraks are Inuit garments that, in shape and form, closely resemble hoodies but usually lack a front pocket and may or may not be decorated with beads. Universally identified with the Inuit, and so with Canada, anoraks provide an awesomely old-school-sounding alternative to "hoodie" and "bunny hug."

REGIONAL DELICACIES

If you could put Canada in your mouth, what would it taste like? Okay, don't answer that question. It was poorly conceived and more poorly phrased. I should have asked, "What are the oral pleasures of Canada?" Hmm—no. I can see some problems with that question too. Well, even though I should probably quit while I'm ahead (recognizing that I've already fallen hopelessly behind), how about, "Canada: A great place to put your tongue." Merde, what am I doing? This section is about eating and drinking. Beyond that, I've already said more than enough.

Bannock

This dense bread is made from flour, baking powder, water or milk, fat and salt. Bannock was a staple for First Nations, traders and explorers in certain parts of the Canadian wilderness. It was awesomely diverse in that you could eat it hot, cold, plain or with a bit of pemmican spread on it. Bannock is so heavy that it was probably also lobbed at unwelcome wild animals or human interlopers, although we are certainly unaware of any "bannock wars."

Brewiss

Pronounced "brooz," this homey East Coast favourite is a stew made from cod, broth, fat, potatoes, herbs and boiled bread (formerly known as "ship's biscuit"). Beloved by locals and visitors alike, brewiss is a humble but hearty meal found simmering on stovetops since the middle of the 18th century and probably much earlier. The stew's awesomeness lies in its heritage, the affection and regard in which it is held, as well as its stick-to-your-ribs good taste.

Cipaille

This hearty meat pie's *awesomeitude* stems not just from its taste but also from its name, which represents a rare occasion in Canadian history when French speakers bastardized an English phrase ("sea pie") into their own distinct expression. Presumably, the original sea pie contained seafood, but the French version contains savoury meats and spices.

Cod

Early explorers of Canada wrote home that they could simply lower a basket into the ocean and haul it up full of squirming cod. Well, we've overfished those waters now, but cod is still a staple of the fishing industry. Desiccated with salt, it will last indefinitely until chucked in a bucket of water to rehydrate it. On the East Coast, when people talk about "fish," they mean cod. For its central part in Canada's economy, its versatility and its fishy savour, we label cod "awesome."

Cod Cheeks

A Maritime delicacy, cod cheeks are just what the name would lead you to think—tender pockets of flesh just under the eye socket of a...cod. There are myriad ways to prepare cod cheeks, but one of the most popular is to pan-fry them either alone or as part of some larger recipe. Cod cheeks are awesome because of their taste and name. What other food can you think of that involves the word "cheeks"?

Cretons

This tasty, spiced-pork spread is a Québec tradition and qualifies for awesomeness because of how surprisingly good it is if you've never eaten it before. You may first regard its sickly grey pallor with suspicion, but after spreading a bit on a piece of toast, its zesty taste can be a revelation. If you have discovered cretons on a visit to

Québec, you may set about trying to find a place to get some in your home province.

Lobster

Before the 1850s, this tasty crustacean wasn't considered food fit for humans, but over the next 50 years or so, it went from being the default staple of impoverished Maritime classes to the must-have food for the upper crust. Quite a rehabilitation for the creature sometimes (and entirely erroneously) called the Cockroach of the Sea.

Pemmican

This age-old First Nations staple is made from ground-up dried meat (usually bison, but also moose, elk or deer) mixed with fat, berries and sometimes other flavouring agents. It is highly nutritious, tastes pretty good, lasts a long time and is portable. First adopted by voyageurs and later by overseas soldiers, pemmican was so awesome on so many fronts that the 1814 seizure of a large pemmican cache by high-handed white settlers resulted in the so-called "Pemmican Wars," battles and engagements that centred around acquiring this useful foodstuff.

Poutine

Hardening arteries have never been more delicious than with Canada's unofficial national food: fries, cheese curds and gravy. Just have a taste to see why poutine counts as awesome. If the taste doesn't convince you (which is unlikely), consider how poutine is alleged to have gotten its name: a customer walks into a Québec diner and asks the proprietor to give him fries, cheese curds and gravy in a paper bag. The owner replies that it will make a *maudite poutine* ("damned mess"), but the owner shovels it all into the bag anyway and hands it over. And so an icon was born.

Prairie Oysters

Who takes bull testicles, cooks them and eats them? Apparently, people on the Prairies. The notion of eating balls doused in some sissy-sounding French sauce called *demi-glace* is not one that leaps to mind when pondering the Prairies' perceived macho culture of cowboy hats, spurred boots and phallic oil rigs. It just goes to show that Canada will not be bound by regional stereotypes—so there.

Salmon

Salmon is delicious and it's good for you, having, as we all now know, a high concentration of omega-3 fatty acids—in other words, the good kind of cholesterol. Salmon was also the primary food source for many West Coast First Nations. These characteristics alone would be enough to make salmon awesome, but also consider that in Canada, you can get almost any form of salmon you want: Atlantic salmon, Pacific salmon, salmon in a tin, smoked salmon, fresh salmon fillets, farm raised salmon, organic salmon and even candied salmon. Whether you're watching the fish majestically (I say, frantically) spawn upstream or enjoying it on a plate in front of you, salmon is a Canadian favourite.

Scrunchions

In effect, scrunchions are crunchy meat curds, and if that alone doesn't make them awesome, I don't know what does. They are bits of animal fat or fish liver suitable either for eating or tossing on the fire as fuel, depending on what sort of animal they come from. Scrunchions can also be fatty cubes of diced pork served as a garnish with fish.

Tourtiere

This delicious meat pie is associated with Québec since it is a favourite dish there. The origins of its name are awesomely confusing. In Québec, passenger pigeons (a common ingredient in the meat pies) were called *tourtes*, leading many to assume that the dish was named after the bird. However, *tourte* also means "pie," which could mean that the pigeons were so called because they were so often made into pies. However, *tourtiere* also means "pie-dish," and this use of the word long predates the advent of pigeon pie. So, it would seem that *tourtiere* is simply named after the dish it is made in. See? I told you it was awesomely confusing.

Un Steamie

This food is Franglais (Québec slang; see "Franglais," p. 75) for a hotdog boiled in steaming water. *Un steamie* is awesome for being a colourful description of a plain dish and far outdistancing *un hotdog* on the interesting scale.

SWEET TREATS

Butter Tarts

Canadians are surprised when they discover that not all nations have (or know about) butter tarts, which is a real shame because of their complete and utter *awesomeneity* (you can only write "awesome" and "awesomeness" so many times before you start making up words). Flavour-wise, butter tarts are similar to pecan pie but contain raisins instead of pecans. Purported to come from a Scottish town called Ecclefechan, butter tarts and their amazing taste eclipse any interest in their murky origins. (Also, take it from me, it's impossible to spell "Ecclefeshan" the same way twice. See?)

Chocolate Bars

The idea of selling chocolate in small, inexpensive bars appears to have originated with New Brunswick's very own Ganong Brothers, manufacturers and purveyors of awesomely delicious chocolate. Legend has it that sometime around 1910, the owners of the company (which had been making chocolate since 1873) thought that small, pre-packaged bars of chocolate might make a good snack for the busy fishermen who plied their trade in and around the Ganongs' home base of St. Stephen, New Brunswick. Should you need further proof of its awesomeness, Ganong was also the first to sell chocolates in a heart-shaped box.

Maple Anything

Whether it's maple syrup, maple-cured ham or those maple leaf–shaped candies made of maple sugar sold in stories all across the nation, maple is a favourite flavour among Canadians and is a "must-try" for many tourists first visiting our shores. We mustn't forget maple-cured bacon, maple-smoked cheese, maple-iced doughnuts, maple-cream doughnuts, maple butter, maple coffee, maple tea, maple popcorn, maple cookies, maple bacon cake and maple syrup on snow—the treat that first introduced the glorious phenomenon of maple to European settlers. Maple flavour is awesome, and we hold this truth to be self-evident.

Nanaimo Bars

Known to make sensitive teeth hurt, these awesomely sweet and delicious squares comprise a foundation of cookie crumbs covered in vanilla buttercream filling and capped with a layer of chocolate. Named for Nanaimo, BC, recipes for these bars circulated for years under various names, including "Women's Institute Bars" and "Mable's Squares." The name doesn't matter, though—it's truly the taste that makes these bars awesome.

Pudding au Chomeur

Literally translated as "unemployment pudding," this Québec dessert is an upside-down cake whose *awesomitude* derives not merely from its tooth-rotting deliciousness, but also its sugges-tion of a stoic determination to enjoy life while enduring its rocky low points. It's a less Pollyanna-esque manifestation of the sentiment, "If life gives you lemons, make lemonade."

Tarte au Sucre (Sugar Pie)

This Acadian dessert comes in slightly different forms, colours and consistencies, but all require a lot of sugar and all of them are pie, which is the only thing you need to know in order to get a mouthwatering notion of the awesomeness involved.

49TH-PARALLEL FAVES

A quick note—not all of these foods are necessarily exclusive to Canada but, for whatever reason, they have found favour with Canadians and, to some extent, have become identified with Canada if only in our own minds. Many of these awesome comestibles and beverages originate in Canada or were invented by Canadians. These are their stories.

BeaverTails

No, we're not talking about the posterior appendage of the world's second largest rodent, but rather the flat pastry confection named after same. The first BeaverTails location was opened in Ottawa's ByWard Market in 1980 by husband and wife entrepreneurs (not to mention patriots) Grant and Pam Hooker. Based on a family recipe, the flat pastry serves as a foundation for a wide range of sweet toppings chosen at the customer's (in)discretion. A high point for the business was U.S. president Barack Obama's visit to the ByWard Market location in 2009.

Fiddleheads

Initially, the tightly furled heads of the ostrich fern were boiled and eaten as a traditional dish in Québec, Atlantic Canada and parts of New England. Now, they are becoming more widely popular, and many Canadians associate fiddleheads with our eastern regions. The vegetables are so named because of their resemblance to the carved scrollwork at the end of a violin's neck.

Ginger Ale (As We Know it)

Drinks called "ginger ale" or "ginger beer" first appeared in the mid-1800s, but it took Toronto chemist John J. McGlaughlin to perfect the milder, "dry" taste of what would come to be known as

"Canada Dry" (a.k.a. The Champagne of Ginger Ale). Introduced in 1904 and patented in 1907, the drink was an instant hit, finding immediate favour with the Governor General and later surpassing its own success as a mixer during Prohibition and the Depression to mask the telltale smell of boozy breath.

Holubtsi

We have to thank Ukrainians not only for kubasa but also for holubtsi, or cabbage rolls. Canadians who enjoy eating can be grateful that when people immigrate looking for a better life, their food generally comes with them.

Kubasa

This particular species of garlic sausage is popular in Canada because of our Ukrainian community. In Alberta, when eaten on a bun like a hotdog, it's called a "kubie" for short, or when pressed into a flat patty and eaten on a hamburger bun, a "kubie sandwich." This is where multiculturalism really pays off—delicious sausage we might not otherwise have known about.

Red Rose Tea

The Red Rose brand is not unique to Canada, but the blend of tea leaves is. The light, mellow taste prompted a famous series of TV commercials in the 1970s and early '80s that featured plummy-sounding English characters lamenting, "Only in Canada, you say? Pity." It's like they're English and they know tea, and our tea is so good that they want it. And they're English. Get it?

Second Cup

This Canadian coffee purveyor is like a much less annoying version of Starbucks and happily predates that company's presence in this country by many years. In the unlikely event that a Tim Hortons in your neighbourhood closes, you can probably find solace at the nearest Second Cup. In fact, a new store may open especially to fill the void. That kind of dedication to ensuring the delivery of sorely needed caffeine is one of the things we call awesome.

Tim Hortons

If you're from Canada, there's no need for me to explain further. If you're new to Canada or visiting, you'll find out soon enough. Despite seesawing alarmingly between Canadian and U.S. majority ownership, Canada's largest food-service retailer outstrips even the mighty McDonalds in number of retail outlets. Sometime in the mid-1990s, someone noticed that a taste for Tim's coffee was sometimes touted as a badge of patriotic pride by ex-pats abroad frustrated at a lack of international presence. Following a successful campaign by Tim's to drive this idea home, the franchise went from being an unacknowledged favourite to being a proudly proclaimed icon.

CONVIVIAL SPIRITS

Baby Duck

Although it is often derided, Baby Duck became a popular and well-known sparkling wine after it was first introduced in 1971. Made in the Niagara region and bearing a non-threatening alcohol content of seven percent, it is a "light" wine. Baby Duck was one of the first homegrown wines to achieve notoriety as being distinctly Canadian.

Beer

Canadians love beer. We're good at making it, and we're *really* good at drinking it. For all that, we still limp in at a rather embarrassing 23rd in the world as far as consumption per capita. The winner is the Czech Republic, with each person drinking, on average, 132 litres of beer every year. Dry-throated Canucks, on the other hand, each quaff a paltry 68 litres per year. And there are 21 other countries in between. Well, anyway, I'm certainly not going to offer up some sort of apology just because we don't drink enough (or am I?). Whatever—beer is awesome in Canada, blah blah blah.

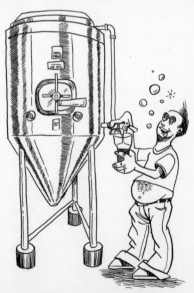

Bloody Caesar

This drink was invented in the 1960s by Calgary bartender Walter Chell. Besides its hearty, piquant taste (often described as going down more like a meal than a beverage), a Caesar is awesome for the bafflement it causes Americans if you try to order one south of the border. If you describe some of the contents—vodka, Worcestershire sauce and Tabasco sauce—to your puzzled Yankee bartender, he or she will reply that you've just described a Bloody Mary minus the tomato juice. This is where you will really blow Tex's mind, when you state that, instead of tomato juice, a Bloody Caesar has *Clamato* juice. That's right—juice made from clams (and tomato juice). There's a reason Canadians are so good at comedy—we drink it for pleasure.

Canadian Club

This whiskey has a reputation as being the preferred drink of tough guys and smooth talkers. Canadian Club (CC) is also the subject of many awesomely unproven legends that have sprung up around its name, most notably that rival American distillers jealous of the brand's success demanded that "Canadian" be added to the name under the assumption that no self-respecting (or jingoistic) American would buy something made in Canada. Seemingly, the distillers in the U.S. failed to realize that few people care where the drink that gets them drunk comes from. As I said, though, this legend is completely unverifiable, which in no way detracts from CC's awesomeness.

Creemore

Brewed in Creemore Springs, Ontario, this tasty lager is free of preservatives and is not pasteurized. It is made using water exclusively from an artesian well (the "spring" in Creemore Springs) located on the brewer's property. Founded in 1987, the Creemore Springs Brewery is a highly successful example of the many microbreweries that began to proliferate in Canada in the 1980s and '90s.

Glenora Distillery

Located on Nova Scotia's scenic Cape Breton Island, Glenora is famous for being the first distillery in Canada to make single-malt whiskey. Their signature Glen Breton Rare is a smooth 10-year-old whiskey that will make you see this rugged corner of Atlantic Canada in a whole new light.

Kokanee

Long brewed in BC, then briefly in Ontario as well, but now only in BC again, Kokanee is named for the Kokanee Glacier. The brewery prominently features Sasquatch as a marketing tool, and its slogan, "It's the beer out here," is bafflingly effective, both igniting the listener's curiosity to (1) go to wherever "here" is, and (2) drink beer there.

Labatt

Founded in 1847 in Ontario, Labatt is the younger but no less successful sibling of Canadian brewing. Probably best known for its ubiquitous "Labatt Blue" brand (named in part for the Winnipeg Blue Bombers CFL team), Labatt also introduced twist-off caps to refillable beer bottles in the 1980s. The family itself also came in for some drama when J.S. Labatt (grandson of the founder, John Kinder Labatt) became a near recluse after he was kidnapped and later released in 1934.

Maudite and La Fin du Monde

Made by Unibroue in Chambly, Québec, both of these beers are Belgian-style ales with strong flavours. "Maudite" (French for "damned") is named for the ghostly voyageurs shown on the label. According to the legend of the Chasse Galerie, voyageurs who botch a deal with the devil must paddle over the treetops for eternity. The name "La Fin du Monde" may derive from European explorers' impression that, upon discovering the east coast of Canada, they had arrived at the "end of the world," or the name may stem from a frantic marketing meeting to name the beer, at which point someone said (in French), "It's not the end of the world."

Molson

Canada's oldest brewery is also the country's second oldest surviving company, period. The Hudson's Bay Company is older, founded in 1670, but Molson was nipping at the Bay's heels a scant 116 years later with the brewery's founding in 1786. Molson is a Canadian icon, having supplied tasty suds to thirsty Canadians for over 200 years (and counting).

Moosehead

Perhaps because its name seems too Canadian to be true, newcomers to Canada can sometimes scarcely believe that we have a beer that is named Moosehead. Founded in 1867 by the Oland family (which still owns the company), Moosehead Brewery is located in Saint John, New Brunswick, and makes a wide variety of delicious beers.

Off-sale Liquor

In BC, Alberta and some northern territories, you can legally buy alcohol at a hotel tavern, take it away (unopened) and drink it somewhere else! Why, you may ask, isn't it this way in all the provinces? Well, we're not sure, but we certainly agree that it ought to be. Besides overall convenience, there's also the trifling bonus of hotels usually being open much later than traditional alcohol retail outlets.

Screech

This incredibly strong rum has become inextricably linked in the national psyche with Newfoundland, which makes sense, because it's made there. The intuitive reason for its naming is probably the correct one—it makes you screech the first time you taste it.

Personally, I would have screeched the first time I tasted it
if the sudden implosion of my mouth had not sucked all the
air out of my lungs. Later, I used the rum to strip the paint off
a 100-year-old chair I was refinishing. Unfortunately, it ate
through the nails, too, and the chair fell apart.

Wine

Before the late 1970s and '80s, if you uttered the phrase "Canadian
wine," it would have made about as much sense as "Australian
French." Since then though, our wines have become pretty good,
with particularly strong showings from British Columbia, Ontario,
Québec and Nova Scotia, each of which boasts several different
wine regions. Canadian wines can be described by using many of
the same adjectives that apply to Canadians themselves: bold,
bright, mellow, low key, robust and occasionally fruity. Cheers!

ART AWESOMENESS

There's a theory that Canadians make good actors and comedians because they bring an "outsider" point of view to all that we see. It makes us sharp observers of the human condition and its attendant complexities and contradictions. In many ways, the same can be said to apply to Canada's distinct vision of the world around us. Canadian artists seem to have a particular genius at painting, drawing and sculpting whatever surrounds them in a way that makes the mundane, magical, and the everyday, exceptional. For Americans and others, viewing Canada through such a lens makes our nation appear as an oddly foreign place, one full of wonders and eccentricities that are, to Canadians, simply part of the fabric of daily life.

Inuit Sculpture

Sadly, for many Canadians, Inuit sculpture has been rendered kitsch by its ubiquitous inclusion in every souvenir shop from Victoria to St. John's and from Inuvik to Toronto. But to see into the past and present culture of an awesome people, you need look no further than the creatures and stories portrayed in the smooth lines and curvilinear shapes of these wondrously wrought figures. Legends, myths and slices of life emerge from jagged chunks of soapstone and slivers of bone as Inuit artisans "carve from the inside out," proceeding with open minds and hearts to see what shapes emerge from the raw material before them.

Totem Poles

Besides being awe-inspiring (and therefore awesome) to look upon, totem poles for the pre-European First Nations were an important way of keeping track of which families had married into a particular clan or tribe. Most families were named after an animal, so the various animals depicted on totem poles were analogous to the families who belonged to a given tribe. This helped to promote exogamy (marrying outside the immediate gene pool) and also made for beautiful and monolithic "family trees" that baffled early Europeans (which, after all, wasn't hard to do). Notable totem poles are scattered throughout BC, but other nations' totems also appear across Canada.

Haida Silversmiths

Although the Haida Nation of BC is often associated with totem poles, its artisans have also found renown as skilled silversmiths, crafting beautiful bracelets, pendants and other jewellery from coolly glistering silver.

Jade

BC has so much jade of such high quality that it's often exported to China. But no matter where the jade is shaped or what it's shaped into, BC jade makes an awesomely beautiful medium to sculpt or carve the visions you see in your mind and feel in your heart (should you be inclined that way—the *sculptorly* way, that is).

Inuit Print Making

I didn't want to put this entry right after "Inuit sculpture" because then it would look like the whole section was going to be about art from north of 60. Anyway, Inuit artists are also well known for their prints, often displaying very simple motifs and techniques, but showcasing a sly sense of humour and flawless composition.

Granville Island

Located in Vancouver, Granville Island is not so much an island as it is a peninsula (though some might be inclined to call it a "spit"). Although it is a popular tourist location known for its scenic backdrop and sprawling food market (both fresh and prepared), the working artists' studios are the reason for the island's fame. You can see painters, sculptors, glass-blowers and other artists as they create their works. In some cases, you can purchase works directly from the artists, or you may prefer to shop among the nearby shops and stalls.

GALLERIES

I fully understand that art belongs in homes and public places as much as it does in galleries, but if you want to fully appreciate a country's capacity to appreciate and contribute to the awesomeness of art, visiting its galleries is a good place to start.

Note: *You may have noticed that for a random assemblage of artistic awesomeness, most of the awesome items in the foregoing section are based in BC or the far north. Don't worry, the rest of the country gets more than a fair shake in the sections that follow, and that's one of the strange anomalies about randomness—sometimes it seems to produce a pattern.*

Vancouver Art Gallery

With a permanent collection of more than 10,000 pieces (in addition to travelling exhibits), you know you're going to get your money's worth. The impressively pillared gallery was once BC's provincial courthouse but now houses (among its many other *objets d'awesome*) the foremost collection of works by Emily Carr (see the "Artists" section).

University of British Columbia Museum of Anthropology

No, it's not exactly an art gallery, but it does boast a breathtaking collection of West Coast First Nations and Aboriginal art. With an extensive collection of totem poles and other artwork, this Vancouver museum's backdrop of mountains and ocean adds another jot of awe to an already awesome package.

Art Gallery of Alberta

Never mind the art inside, the building itself is a swirling marriage of glass and metal featuring an undulating 190-metre steel ribbon that the gallery's website says, "references the forms of the North Saskatchewan River and aurora borealis." Really, though, once you've decided to create a big, bendy, metal structure, does it really matter why? The swirling miasma continues inside the Edmonton gallery, too, with nary a straight line nor a square edge in sight.

Winnipeg Art Gallery

As if the world's largest collection of Inuit art wasn't awesome enough, the WAG also has an impressive collection of Gothic, Renaissance and European art. Founded in 1912 as Canada's first civic art gallery, the WAG now occupies an awesomely mod-looking building that resembles a sleek grey wedge of stone building blocks.

National Gallery

If you're afraid of spiders, you may want to approach Ottawa's National Gallery with caution—outside is a massive bronze sculpture of a spider, entitled *Maman* (mother), that is more than 9 metres tall and 10 metres wide. Then there's the amazing art inside. Housing a truly world-class collection of art from Canadian greats the Group of Seven to Renaissance masters and all styles before or since, the National Gallery (and its giant spider) is awesome in every sense of the word.

Art Gallery of Ontario

Befronted by a massive abstract bronze (a Henry Moore) and featuring Frank Gehry's (see p. 211) new façade (his first Canadian commission), Toronto's AGO makes it easy to miss the art for the gallery. It's well worth a look inside, however, because it has something for everyone, including an entire room of shipbuilder's models, some of which are hundreds of years old.

Musée d'Art Contemporain

Located in Montréal, the Museum of Contemporary Art is the only facility of its scale in Canada to focus solely on modern art, so don't expect to see any Renaissance masters. Wide-open interior spaces and a sculpture garden encourage a contemplative state of mind, the better to appreciate the awesome art.

Musée des Beaux Arts

So large that it is housed in two completely separate buildings across the street from one another, Montréal's Musée des Beaux Arts is Québec's first and most extensive public art collection. The newer wing, the Jean-Noel Desmarais Pavilion, has a modern façade and exhibits works ranging from the Middle Ages to the present day. The older arm, the Michal and Renata Hornstein Pavilion, is dedicated to Canadiana, which is awesome in its own right.

ARTISTS

Emily Carr (1871–1945)

Painter and writer Emily Carr is an inspiration to all of the late bloomers out there—she didn't receive any recognition until she was 57 and had barely painted in the preceding 15 years. Her fascination with First Nations totem poles and abandoned villages fused with a passion for the Canadian landscape to the point that the Group of Seven regarded her as an artist of their own stature, triggering another burst of productivity in the third act of her life. After a heart attack reduced her capacity to paint, she turned to writing and penned a series of well-received books. She is awesome in so many ways that it's difficult to choose just one.

Group of Seven

If Tom Thomson was the first artist to realize that the Canadian landscape looked more itself when painted in a vividly impressionistic style, then the Group of Seven artists took this realization and ran with it, setting out to forge a Canadian school of painting—and succeeding. The Group of Seven were Franklin Carmichael (1890–1945), Lawren Harris (1885–1970), A.Y. Jackson (1882–1972), Frank Johnston (1888–1949), Arthur Lismer (1885–1969), J.E.H. MacDonald (1873–1932) and Frederick Varley (1881–1969).

Indian Group of Seven

Banding together in 1973, this group of Aboriginal artists joined forces to make the point that their work should be assessed on its merit as art and not the artists' ethnography. But the press quickly dubbed them the Indian Group of Seven. They were Jackson Beardy (1944–84), Alex Janvier (b. 1935), Eddy Cobiness (1933–66), Norval Morrisseau (1932–2007), Daphne Odjig (b. 1919), Carl Ray (1943–78) and Joseph Sanchez (b. 1948).

Yousuf Karsh (1908–2002)

Arguably the world's foremost photographic portraitist, Karsh is famous for pulling a cigar out of Winston Churchill's lips moments before taking a picture claimed to be the most reproduced photo portrait on earth. Some of the other people whose portraits were taken by Karsh include Pablo Picasso, Georgia O'Keefe, George Bernard Shaw, Frank Lloyd Wright, Muhammad Ali, John F. Kennedy, Jacqueline Kennedy, Joan Crawford, Joan Baez, Carl Jung, Chuck Jones, Andy Warhol, Ernest Hemingway, Clark Gable, Dwight D. Eisenhower, the members of Rush, Humphrey Bogart and Albert Einstein, to name just a few.

Tom Thomson (1877–1917)

As far as Canadian painters go, Tom Thomson is the total package.
He was first to paint the Canadian landscape in the bold brush-
strokes of (post-) impressionism, he was a humble, temperamental
artist who loved nothing more than canoeing and camping in
Algonquin park, he was good looking and he died under circumstances that have only become more mysterious as time passes.
If you are looking for a charismatic figure to embody the birth of
a fledgling Canadian school of art, Tom Thomson is it (see also
"Group of Seven").

Bill Reid (1920–98)

Bill Reid was a Haida woodcarver and sculptor who is credited with keeping alive a First Nations style of sculpture and art following World War II. His major works are immediately recognizable to most Canadians, having appeared in galleries, on posters and on money. From 2004 to 2012, Reid's sculpture *Raven and the First Men* appeared on the obverse of the $20 bill. Much of Aboriginal art's ongoing popularity is largely because of Reid's talent and passion.

Robert Bateman (b. 1930)

Canada's foremost realist painter of nature is also an environmental advocate. Still, it's the photographic realism and clarity of his meticulously composed nature and wildlife scenes that have earned him the justifiably awesome reputation he enjoys. That he looks kind of like Robert Redford doesn't hurt, either. If you're too young to know who Robert Redford is, go look it up.

Ken Danby (1940–2007)

To understand why Ken Danby is included in a book of awesome things about Canada, just look at one of his many paintings. Falling squarely into the realm of "magic realism," Danby's works are sometimes mistaken for beautifully composed photographs. His most famous work *At the Crease* shows a hockey goalie waiting and alert in front of goalposts.

ADVOCATES AND DO-GOODERS

Canadians are awesomely proactive. When we see a wrong, an injustice or just a broken situation that needs mending, Canucks are ready to step up. Sometimes we're out to improve the world in big, bold and seemingly impossible ways, but in other instances, we're out to address individual wrongs or simply help one another. Whatever the cause, whatever the challenge, we're a nation that not only nurtures big-hearted spirits, but welcomes them as well. (PS: Tommy Douglas is covered in a different section.)

Josiah Henson (1789–1883)

An escaped slave from the U.S., Henson fled north to Canada and bought a plot of land near Dawn Township, Ontario. It was a haven for other escaped slaves and soon became the centre of a small but successful logging business that employed many in the town. Henson published a famous memoir, served as a preacher, advocated for the abolition of slavery and is generally regarded as the model for the titular character of Harriet Beecher Stowe's novel of the Underground Railway, *Uncle Tom's Cabin*.

Mary Ann Shadd (1823–93)

Fleeing from slavery in the U.S., Shadd founded and published an abolitionist newspaper, *The Provincial Freeman*, in Windsor, Ontario, and later, in Toronto. She was the first female publisher in Canada and the first black female publisher in North America. In a time when many former slaves were in favour of segregation, Shadd was firmly against it, forming a racially integrated school, also in Windsor. With the end of the Civil War, she returned to the U.S. and went on to become the second black woman in the U.S. to earn a law degree.

Grey Owl (1888–1938)

An alcoholic bigamist fraudster is awesome? Well, when he's Grey Owl, yes. Seemingly of Scots-Apache heritage, Grey Owl wrote influential and bestselling books that established him as the father of the conservation movement, advocating the preservation of vanishing habitats. Soon he was hobnobbing with heads of state and royalty. But when he died, it emerged that "Grey Owl" had really been a pale-faced limey named Archie Belaney who drank too much and was married to more than one woman at the same time. Grey Owl's influence waned after his death, but his ideas were rediscovered a generation later, contributing to the founding of the modern environmental movement.

Chief Dan George (1899–1981)

Discovered as an actor when he was 60, Dan George got his start in TV and went on to be nominated for an Academy Award for the 1970 film *Little Big Man.* He also published several well-received works of prose poetry and recited his famous "Lament for Confederation" at Expo '67. Part of George's awesomeness was in his intent as an actor—he played parts that portrayed Aboriginal characters not as confrontational "Cowboys and Injuns" stereotypes, but as positive characters with human kindnesses, frailties and greatness of heart.

Dr. Mary Jackson (1904–2000)

Trained as a doctor in England, Mary Jackson responded to a newspaper ad looking for doctors in rural Alberta. Soon she was a frontier doctor in Battle River Prairie. She travelled by horse, dogsled and on foot to reach her far-flung patients, many of whom had no money with which to pay her, so they offered her food or barter in return for treatment. Over a long and literally active professional life, Jackson set broken bones, delivered babies and treated lumberjacks with axe wounds, fuelled by her passion rather than monetary reward or recognition.

June Callwood (1924–2007)

Writer, broadcaster and social activist, June Callwood led a busy, prolific and productive life that was guided by compassion and shaped by hard work. Author of 30 books, she also helped found Digger House (a shelter for homeless youth), Nellie's (a shelter for women in crisis), Jessie's Centre (for pregnant teens and young parents) and Casey House (an AIDS hospice named for her youngest son, killed in a motorcycle accident). She was also a qualified airplane and glider pilot. Just writing this makes me want to do more with my life and do it better.

David Suzuki (b. 1936)

Geneticist, broadcaster and passionate advocate for planet earth, Suzuki is renowned at home and abroad as a scientist and media presenter of immense talent and ability. Creator of CBC Radio's *Quirks and Quarks* and later, CBC television's *The Nature of Things*, Suzuki believes that greater awareness of science contributes positively to both institutional policies and society in general. The many ways and areas in which he is awesome would take far too long to enumerate.

Terry Fox (1958–81)

Having lost his right leg to cancer when he was 18, BC's Terry Fox embarked on a cross-Canada run a few years later to raise money for cancer research. Starting out from St. John's, Newfoundland, in August 1980, he completed more than 5000 kilometres of his trek before the spread of cancer to his lungs forced him to quit in Thunder Bay, Ontario. He died in June 1981, but not before he had raised more than $1 million for cancer research, inspired Canadians from coast to coast and laid the groundwork for the ongoing fundraising runs that bear his name. If Terry Fox had been diagnosed with cancer today, the treatment available might have saved him—cancer research works.

Canadian Voice of Women for Peace

Founded in 1960, this anti-nuclear group held the first-ever international peace conference in 1962. The members are also notable for a campaign to collect baby teeth from all across North America in order to show that they contained significant amounts of the radioactive isotope strontium-90, which enters the atmosphere after nuclear explosions.

Randy Stoltmann (1962–94)

An interest in finding record-sized trees in BC's Stanley Park led Randy Stoltmann to become an early advocate of "old-growth value," the idea that the oldest trees in an environment should be nurtured and respected as opposed to simply being cut down for commerce or industry. He published three books and wrote numerous articles as well as helping to construct many trails for the greater enjoyment of BC's parks and woodland areas. He was killed in an avalanche in 1994. A parcel of land along the Elaho River in BC is now named the Stoltmann Wilderness Area.

Craig Kielburger (b. 1982)

Kielburger is the founder of Free the Children, an international youth advocacy and volunteer group that works on a model of "children helping children." He is also the founder of Me to We, a for-profit group that sells ethically sound products and donates half of the proceeds to Free the Children. Kielburger is a shining example of a Canadian who is forward-looking, proactive and positive.

Neil Pasricha

Down (but not out) after the breakup of his marriage and the loss of a close friend, Torontonian Pasricha started a blog in 2008 (1000AwesomeThings.com) that listed a miscellany of life's little awesome moments, ranging from the smell of rain on a hot sidewalk to having someone throw a blanket over you as you're about to fall asleep. One Webby Award and two bestselling books later, Pasricha's observations continue to inspire and hearten the masses.

Max Sidorov

In June 2012, the world watched in horror as Karen Klein, a 68-year-old school bus monitor in the U.S., was bullied to tears by teen bus riders on a trip home. The teens themselves then posted the video to YouTube. Toronto graduate student Max Sidorov was horrified and launched an online appeal for money through the fundraising site Indiegogo. Sidorov's goal was to raise $5000 to send Klein on a vacation. Donors wound up contributing more than $700,000, and Sidorov (along with Klein) went on to launch an anti-bullying campaign called 7 Million Acts of Love.

STRENGTHENING THE SOCIAL FABRIC

Underground Railway

Canadians typically like to ignore that slavery existed in Canada, but because our economy was not based on plantation agriculture (as in the U.S.), slavery did not become entrenched. Following Canadian legislation in 1793, any slave that set foot in Canada became a free person (though slavery would not be abolished in the British Empire until 1834). This law opened the door for the Underground Railway, a secret route for escaped U.S. slaves to make their way north to Canada, which saw its period of peak use between 1850 and 1860. It wasn't really a railway, and it wasn't really underground, but it was awesome.

Negotiating

Both at home and abroad, Canadians enjoy the reputation of being fair and impartial negotiators—sort of the anti–Fox News. Be it social strife, labour unrest or major sports league negotia-tions, you're likely to find one or more Canucks at the table, silently wishing for a Tim Hortons coffee as they maintain their manners with openness and fairness.

Telemiracle Marathon

In 1977, Kinsmen in Saskatchewan produced a 20-hour TV mara-thon to raise money for people with special needs. It continues today, pulling in more than $3 million each year and sitting at a running total of about $63 million.

Harold Hacket

In 1996, Harold Hacket of Tignish, Newfoundland, began putting messages in bottles and casting them into the ocean. Since then, he has "sent" nearly 5000 bottle messages and has received more than 3000 responses, usually by post. What an awesome way to make friends and "meet" new people.

Project Naming

From the late 1800s to the 1950s, whenever photographs were taken of Inuit in Canada's far north, the predominantly white photographers rarely identified any of their subjects. Project Naming, started in 2001, is a joint effort between Nunavut Sivuniksavut (a college training program in Ottawa) and Library and Archives Canada to identify as many of the individuals and places shown in these photos as possible. Elders in far-flung communities have so far identified hundreds of people and places, putting names and faces to their heritage.

The People of Gander, Newfoundland

In 2001, when 5000 to 10,000 U.S. travellers were stranded in Gander following airport closures in the wake of the September 11 terrorist attacks, Ganderians opened their hearts, homes and any extra space to the unexpected visitors. Sometimes just doing the right thing is the awesome thing to do.

The Red Paper Clip

On July 12, 2005, Montréaler Kyle Macdonald started the website OneRedPaperClip.com. His goal was to see what he could trade for something truly insignificant—a red paper clip. First, he traded it for a fish-shaped pen and then a ceramic doorknob, but exactly one year and 14 trades later, Macdonald became the proud owner of a house in Kipling, Saskatchewan!

CANADA WAS HERE

*Canada, and Canadians, tend to pop up in the unlikeliest
of places. Whether they're wearing stereotypical Mountie
(see p. 80) garb or futuristic space uniforms, Canadians
have irresistibly intruded into the popular culture of that
nation to the south, known to some of its own inhabitants
as the United States of "Uhmurrika." You'll find Canucks
in places both surprising and predictable.*

Rose Marie

This popular 1924 operetta was filmed no less than three times.
Set in the Canadian Rockies and parts of Québec, many see it
as an early representation of Canada as a land of snow, rugged
terrain, noble Mounties, warm-hearted French Canadians and
a whole raft of other stereotypes that the subsequent filmed
versions certainly helped to spread and perpetuate.

Sergeant Preston of the Yukon

After starting out as a 1938 U.S. radio show called *Challenge of
the Yukon*, the name was changed to *Sergeant Preston of the Yukon*
in 1951 before the show made the move to TV, airing on CBS
from 1955 to 1958. As far as creating and entrenching stereotypes goes, *Sergeant Preston* picks up where *Rose Marie* left off.
The titular character is an upright Mountie who travels the
snowy plains by dogsled, ably assisted by his closest friend,
an excellent husky named King.

Dudley Do-Right

Although the character was created around 1948, this
well-intentioned but obliviously incompetent Mountie really
came into his own as a character in the animated TV series
Rocky and Bullwinkle, starting in 1961 and later appeared in

his own series of short cartoons. The character painted a picture of the Mounties as being well meaning but hopelessly clueless in the workings of the real world.

Wolverine

Everyone's favourite mutant from the *X-Men* comics and movies is Canadian, having been born as James Howlett in the 1880s in Alberta. The 2000 film *X-Men* properly paid tribute to his heritage with the character of Rogue first encountering Wolverine in a rough tavern in the far north, where a blue $5 bill with Wilfrid Laurier on it can be prominently seen in the tips jar.

Alpha Flight

Originally created by Marvel comics as part of a backstory for Wolverine, Alpha Flight became "Canada's answer to the Avengers," with their own comic featuring a team of superpowered beings who were all Canucks. True to form, an early issue opened with an arctic research team bemoaning the fact that Ottawa had cut their funding. On the downside, the U.S. artists at Marvel couldn't draw the Canadian flag to save their lives.

James Bond

He still hasn't visited Canada in any movies, but in the short story *For Your Eyes Only*, the literary 007 flies into Montréal on his way to Ottawa to sneak into the U.S. for a covert kill. And in the novel *The Spy Who Loved Me*, the narrator (later banged by Bond), Vivien Michelle, is a French Canadian.

Sir Henry Baskerville

In the book *The Hound of the Baskervilles*, Sherlock Holmes' most famous client, Sir Henry Baskerville, has just returned to England after farming in Canada, where he purchased some new boots from a boot maker in Toronto named "Meyers."

The Scarlet Claw

Getting a leg up on the cinematic James Bond, on celluloid at least, Sherlock Holmes made it to Canada in the 1944 Basil Rathbone–starrer *The Scarlet Claw*, set in a small fictional Québec village called La Mort Rouge.

Winnie the Pooh

Author A.A. Milne found the name for the world's most famous bear when he visited the London Zoo with his son, Christopher Robin. They saw a bear that had been left behind as the unofficial mascot of Canadian soldiers overseas in World War I. The bear had been named "Winnipeg"—"Winnie" for short.

Elmer Fudd

Bugs Bunny's frequent nemesis, Elmer Fudd, appears as
a Mountie that is out to get his rabbit in the 1942 short
Fresh Hare.

20,000 Leagues Under the Sea

The Jules Verne classic of underwater adventure features a central
character named Ned Land, who is a French Canadian harpooner.

Sergeant Pepper's Lonely Hearts Club Band

Arguably The Beatles' most famous album, *Sergeant Pepper's* was
released in 1967 and contains two Canadian references. Most
noticeably, in the album's gatefold, Paul McCartney's blue satin
frock coat has an Ontario Provincial Police (OPP) badge sewn
onto it. And one of the many people shown in the cover collage
is Canadian-born dancer Bobby Breen, visible as a rather disem-
bodied head over George Harrison's left shoulder.

John Lennon

John not only staged one of his infamous 1969 "Bed-Ins" with
Yoko Ono in Montréal's Queen Elizabeth Hotel, but a few months
later, the couple also met with then Prime Minister Pierre Trudeau
for nearly an hour. Yoko said Trudeau was a "beautiful" person,
and Lennon opined, "If all politicians were like Mr. Trudeau,
there would be world peace." Yeah, yeah, yeah.

Bruce Lee

What appears to be the only surviving in-depth television interview of martial arts master and actor Bruce Lee was conducted
by none other than Canada's own Pierre Berton, when the latter's
TV program *The Pierre Berton Show* visited Hong Kong in 1971.

Bob and Doug McKenzie

Portrayed by Dave Thomas (Doug) and Rick Moranis (Bob),
Canada's most famously self-referential exports were created in
1980 when the CBC, in its infinite wisdom, asked the writers of
SCTV for two additional minutes of content that was distinctly
Canadian—this on a show written, performed and produced
by Canadians in Canada. Creating the characters as a metaphorically raised middle finger to the CBC, Thomas and Moranis were
shocked when the McKenzie Brothers became *SCTV*'s most popular segment, spawning two albums and a movie.

Brother Bear

So great was the McKenzie Brothers' popularity that, in the 2003
Disney movie *Brother Bear,* Dave Thomas and Rick Moranis
voiced a pair of brethren moose, who sounded suspiciously like
Bob and Doug McKenzie.

The Simpsons

Due in part, perhaps, to creator Matt Groening's father being a Canadian, not to mention a revolving door of Canadian staff writers, TV's longest running sitcom is rife with Canadian references so numerous it is impossible to include them all. But here are a few examples, in no particular order: Bart lies about an upcoming road trip by telling his family that he will be competing at the National Grammar Rodeo in Calgary; the family attends the 2010 Olympics in Vancouver; the Sea Captain espouses the virtues of "O Canada" as a national anthem; and the National Film Board of Canada is listed as the producer of an awful vampire film.

Betty and Veronica

When they weren't busy competing for the affections of their thatch-headed friend, Archie Andrews, these two comicbook characters found time to drop by West Edmonton Mall in the "Betty and Veronica Spectacular" (*Comic Digest*, 1991).

South Park

Among many other references to Canada on the U.S. animated comedy, *South Park,* the most notable is probably from the 1999 movie *South Park: Bigger, Longer and Uncut,* in which parents of the town's rude children, instead of admitting to their own deficiencies as parents, choose to "Blame Canada" in an elaborate musical number of the same name.

News Radio

This U.S. sitcom starred Canadian actor and comedian Dave Foley as Dave Nelson, the cool-headed overseer of the zany staff of a New York talk-radio station. In one episode, Dave's character, previously thought to be from Wisconsin, is revealed as having been born in Canada.

Star Trek

Besides Captain Kirk himself—or rather, William Shatner, who portrays him and is a Canuck (and let's not forget Scotty, played by James Doohan)—the *Star Trek* franchise has many other Canadian connections. In the original series' classic episode, "The Trouble with Tribbles," Mr. Spock mentions that the ancestor of a special kind of grain was first grown in Canada. *Star Trek: The Next Generation*'s season-two episode, "Contagion," features Toronto City Hall in a montage of "futuristic"-looking buildings shown in a sort of dimensional portal. In *Deep Space Nine*'s fifth-season episode, "Blaze of Glory," a character is proud of his antique Canadian dollar coin, referring to it as his "lucky loonie."

MIXED BAG OF MARVELS

We take a short break from the themed sections to list this compact cross-section of awesomeness that otherwise defies categorization, including real-life national icons, a hockey phenomenon that doesn't appear to be going anywhere soon and a pair of superheroes.

Dionne Quintuplets

The awesomeness of the Quints' survival is matched only by the shameful manner of their exploitation and tragic home life. Born in 1934, the Quints instantly became famous as the first set of quintuplets known to have survived more than a few days past birth (a sixth fetus miscarried). The Government of Ontario swiftly stepped in and declared the Quints wards of the state, subsequently exploiting the five sisters as a tourist attraction and making mascots out of them. There was even an outlandish plan to send the little girls to live at Casa Loma in Toronto. When the Quints were nine, their parents won custody once more, and the five siblings endured a home life of abuse and rejection. They were, however, a beacon of hope and brightness in the midst of the Depression, not just for Canadians but also for others around the world.

Nelvana of the Northern Lights

Created in 1941 by cartoonist Adrian Dingle, Nelvana of the Northern Lights was the first Canadian superhero and one of the first female superheroes, making her debut before Wonder Woman. Nelvana lived among the Inuit, and her powers included using the aurora borealis as a path to travel at light speed to wherever she wanted to go. The Canadian animation company, Nelvana (see p. 174), is named after her.

Captain Canuck

First appearing on newsstands in 1975, the *Captain Canuck* comic has been sporadically published on and off since then. Captain Canuck is a Captain America–like figure but is dressed in red and white, as opposed to red, white and blue.

Superman

This superhero is so well known now that it almost seems redundant to include it, but yes, the Man of Steel was created, in part, by a Canadian. Jerry Siegel and Joe Shuster came up with the idea of Superman. Shuster was from Toronto and, incidentally, was a cousin to comedian Frank Shuster of (Johnny) Wayne and Shuster fame. Shuster always claimed that *The Daily Planet*, where Superman's alter ego, mild-mannered Clark Kent worked as a reporter, was modelled on *The Toronto Star*.

Hockey Zombies

Come NHL playoff time, you will see inarticulately roaring hordes roaming the streets and occasionally rioting, setting vehicles on fire and generally pillaging. They usually wear hockey jerseys and have grotesquely painted faces. They cannot be reasoned with nor controlled. Their brains have been eaten. These are hockey zombies. Canada invented them.

MAPLE LEAF METTLE

The title of this section pretty much says it all. We certainly want to acknowledge the bravery and courage of our troops but, on the other hand, as most of them would likely be the first to admit, war itself is not awesome.

Peacekeeping

Partly by choice, but mainly by necessity, Canada opts to use its armed forces primarily for peacekeeping and rescue operations. For whatever the reason, we call this a choice of astonishing sanity in the current world climate.

World Wars

A contentious point of awesomeness to say the least, but we did our part in both World Wars I and II.

One Brave Goat

Known as Sergeant Bill, this omnivorous goat was shipped overseas during World War I as a mascot for the Fifth Canadian Infantry Battalion. The goat soon endeared himself to the enlisted men by eating the roll call and head butting officers, but Bill truly earned his stripes when he saved a soldier's life by butting him into a trench just before a German shell detonated nearby.

Vimy Ridge

This 1917 offensive of World War I in France saw four Canadian divisions fight together for the first time—and not merely as cohorts to British forces. The Canadian Corps took the ridge in a resounding success (and at a cost of nearly 4000 dead), regarded ever since with great national pride.

Passchendaele

Sometimes called "Canada's other Vimy Ridge" (see above), the Battle of Passchendaele was a victory for Canada, succeeding where other Allied forces had failed, but it came at a great cost, with 15,000 dead or wounded. The ridge was later retaken by the Germans, but from then on, Canadian troops were among the most feared forces of World War I.

Liberated Holland During World War II

This feat is mentioned in part for its inherent awesomeness and partly for the trickle-down awesomeness of the continued friendly relations between the Netherlands and Canada.

Project Habakkuk

During World War II, Lord Mountbatten, chief of combined operations, investigated the idea of building giant ships out of ice and wood pulp to serve as both troop transports and aircraft carriers. Mountbatten commissioned a prototype, to be built on the shores of Patricia Lake in Alberta, near Jasper. Disguised with a metal roof to make it look like a boathouse, the ice ship was partially built, but multiple problems and cost overruns forced Project Habakkuk to be scrapped. How's that for an awesomely cockamamie wartime scheme (that just might have worked)?

Deadly Snipers

Since World War II, Canadians have earned renown as deadly snipers. Perhaps it's because our country is so large that Canadians are good at shooting at faraway targets.

German POW Camps

During World War II, about 40 prisoner-of-war camps were scattered across Canada, mainly in Québec, Ontario and Alberta. So humane were the conditions in the camps that, according to anecdotal evidence, prisoners rarely tried to escape (besides, they were in the middle of the Canadian wilderness, with part of a continent, all of an ocean and the end of the war between them and home).

Norman Bethune (1890–1939)

This surgeon and inventor of medical devices is remembered today for becoming a communist and working tirelessly in China as a doctor in the communist army. He designed and organized the world's first mobile medical unit in order to perform blood transfusions on the front.

Avro Arrow

This legendary supersonic jet fighter, designed and built by Canadians, was 20 years ahead of its time. The program and most of the existing aircraft were controversially scrapped by John Diefenbaker's government in 1959. It remains an awesome "what-if" (see p. 302) in Canadian history.

War in Iraq

When the U.S. invaded Iraq in 2003, looking for non-existent weapons of mass destruction (WMDs), Canada was on the right side of the line and refused to participate because there was simply no evidence whatsoever that Iraq had any WMDs. No WMDs were ever found.

Sea Kings

The awesome here is the brave pilots and crews who kept these aged helicopters running from 1963 to the early 2000s. So infamously obsolete were these aircraft that, in recent years, cynics have created gag flight badges that read, "Flying yesterday's aircraft today."

AWESOME "AGENTS"

Laura Secord (1775–1868)

This much-mythologized figure in Canadian history did indeed walk 30 kilometres to warn the British of an impending American attack during the War of 1812. How she learned of the attack and whether or not the British already knew about it from First Nations scouts remains in question. In 1913, an enterprising chocolatier chose to name his company after her, and so Laura Secord Chocolates was born.

Frank Zaneth (1890–1971)

In the 1920s and '30s, Frank Zaneth (born Franco Zanetti) was probably the RCMP's most active and successful undercover agent. In exploit after exploit, he donned disguises and went up against radicals, labour agitators, bootleggers and mob bosses. To keep his identity secret, he was only ever referred to in reports as "Operative No. 1."

Sir William Stephenson (1896–1989)

Millionaire inventor turns spymaster—does it get any better? The exact details of Stephenson's espionage role during World War II remain shrouded in uncertainty—how much of what people said he did, did he actually do? Although he was probably not known as "Intrepid" as is so often claimed, Stephenson was key to creation of the now famous Camp X school for spies near Whitby, Ontario.

THE POLITICS OF PEOPLE

Mary Brant (c. 1736–96)

Mary Brant (a.k.a. Konwatsi'tsiaiénni) was an influential Mohawk in the Six Nations confederacy in Ontario. Her intelligence and leadership were instrumental in convincing the Six Nations to remain loyal to the British during the American Revolution.

William Lyon Mackenzie (1795–1861)

One of the leaders of the Rebellion of 1837, Mackenzie was also a newspaper publisher, politician, firebrand and all-round pain in neck for the Family Compact, the predominantly Protestant clique that ruled Toronto for most of the 19th century. His ghost may or may not haunt the house that was his final home (now open to the public as a museum) on Toronto's Bond Street.

Sir Charles Tupper (1821–1914)

Chuck Tupp, as I like to call him, was both the oldest and shortest serving prime minister in Canadian history, holding office for just 69 days in 1896 when he was 74 years old!

Thomas D'Arcy McGee (1825–68)

Generally regarded as the most eloquent of the Fathers of Confederation, McGee was also a prolific writer, poet and public speaker. Unfortunately, he's also one of the few Canadian politicians to be assassinated. It's awesome that there have been so few, but sad that he is one of them.

Amor de Cosmos (1825–97)

It is baffling to me that more people haven't heard of Amor de Cosmos. He was the premier of BC from 1872 to 1874, having changed his name from William Alexander Smith some 20 years previously in, where else, California. You'd think that any premier whose name meant "Love of the Universe," especially one who governed at the end of the 19th century, would get a bit more ink. Seriously—why is he not the most famous premier in the history of Canada?

Gabriel Dumont (1837–1906)

This Métis leader from Saskatchewan was among the first to notice and accept that the days of hunting buffalo were numbered and that his remarkable skills as a horseman, marksman and canoeist would soon be irrelevant. A brave warrior for his people, he was also a good negotiator and a representative in various provisional governments.

Louis Riel (1844–85)

A controversial figure to this day, Riel awesomely led the Métis in two separate armed resistances against the encroachment of white settlers (in 1869 and 1885). He was the founder of the province of Manitoba, and the government of the day hanged him for it (and other crimes, not least of which was choosing to execute surveyor and militiaman Thomas Scott).

William Lyon Mackenzie King (1874–1950)

Grandson of William Lyon Mackenzie, King was prime minister of Canada for 22 years on and off (but mainly on, obviously). Besides communing with the spirits via séances for the last 25 years of his life, he also kept a diary, in which he wrote or dictated nearly every day for 57 years. All of that adds up to a healthy awesome quotient.

Lester B. Pearson (1897–1972)

Pearson is awesome not for being prime minister of Canada from 1963 to 1968, but rather for his 1956 suggestion to the UN to create the first peacekeeping force to monitor the Suez Canal Crisis. He was awarded the Nobel Peace Prize in 1957 for this visionary notion.

Ellen Fairclough (1905–2004)

Fairclough was Canada's first female cabinet minister, appointed Secretary of State when John Diefenbaker came to power in 1957. She was also Canada's first woman Acting Prime Minister for one day in 1958, meaning that, in some ways, Fairclough beat Kim Campbell to the finish line by more than 35 years.

Kim Campbell (b. 1947)

Canada's first female prime minister was in office for just over four months in 1993, which means she didn't exactly get much of a chance to leave her mark.

Tommy Douglas (1904–86)

The father of socialized medicine in Canada also brought democratic socialist government to the mainstream in Canada through the formation of the CCF (Co-operative Commonwealth Federation), the progenitor of the NDP. He was also a good boxer.

Sheila Copps (b. 1952)

For many years a prominent, outspoken and able member of the Liberal Party, Copps was unmatched in her widely admired ability to be a perpetual thorn in the side of any Progressive Conservative government that may have been within spitting distance.

TALKING CANUCK

After 400 years of clashing cultures, languages, belief systems, beer preferences and hockey teams, Canada has produced a vibrant language of its own, often unintelligible to newcomers, but all the more inviting and mysterious for it. If you were a recent immigrant to these shores (or even this side of the border), what might you think upon hearing the following?

Canadian Spelling

I'm not going to drag this out, but I'm referring to the way we spell the following words in contrast to our southern neighbours: "colour," not "color"; "centre," not "center"; "grey," not "gray"; and "cheque," not "check." Thank you and good night.

Chimo

In the years surrounding Canada's centennial in 1967, this Inuit greeting, given to mean either "Hello" or "Are you friendly?" briefly found currency in non-Inuit circles as a friendly and distinctly Canadian salute to either friends or strangers. It was also adopted as the cheer of the Canadian Military Engineers.

Chinook Jargon

This was an informal language that sprang up in 19th-century British Columbia to accommodate Nootka, Salish, French and English traders. From this jargon comes another famous Canadianism, "Give 'er snoose!" to exhort someone to attend to the task at hand with great ardour, which is a strange phrase, since *snoose* is Chinook jargon for "chewing tobacco."

Depanneur

In Québec, a *depanneur* (or "dep") is a variety store. People who have grown up or lived in Québec often fondly carry over the word when they move to another province.

Double-double

Probably the most famous Canadianism after "eh" (see below), "double-double" is shorthand when ordering coffee (or tea for that matter) for "two creams and two sugars." A possibly apocryphal story concerns American soldiers overhearing two Canadians ordering coffee at the temporary Tim Hortons in Afghanistan and assuming that "double-double" was some sort of code, which after all, strictly speaking, it is.

Eh

Use of this little flavouring phrase tagged on at the end of an utterance varies across the years and generations, according to geography and socioeconomic status. It is an easily brayed stereotype, often heard issuing from the lips of Americans and some other nationalities upon hearing that one is a Canadian. In all fairness, you hear it falling unironically from Canadian mouths the most of all.

Franglais

A mixture of French and English, either seamless or ragged; for example, in the phrase, "*Bon* weekend" or "I'm going to the *depanneur*." "Franglais" is a portmanteau of two French words: *Français* ("French") and *Anglais* ("English")—the languages, not the nationalities. One unfortunate example of Franglais is the name LaRue Walker, which means "street walker" in French.

Give 'er

Short for "Give 'er snoose" (see "Chinook Jargon"), this can mean, "Get your back into it," literally or metaphorically, or more succinctly, "Go for it." If you happen to walk past a couple necking in a car, shout out, "Give 'er!" The couple will probably be too busy to notice your presence, but it's fun to do anyway.

"He Shoots, He Scores!"

First springing from the lips of hockey commentator Foster Hewitt, this expression, uttered with frenzied enthusiasm, may be comfortably used whenever a person has set out to do something and succeeded handsomely or against unlikely odds.

Hoser

This generic insult, meaning variously "fool," "loser" or "jerk," was at it its most popular in the early 1980s following the release of the McKenzie Brothers album *Great White North*. Before that, "to get hosed" was a real insult in Atlantic Canada, referring to someone on the losing end of a game or situation. Seldom heard nowadays, "hoser," because of its nostalgic value, will usually coax a grin out of anyone within earshot, including the person at whom it is directed.

Newfoundland English

Completely deserving of the many popular and scholarly works it has spawned, Newfoundland English is rightly regarded as one of Canada's national treasures. It has given us such colourful phrases as: "bare-legged tea" (tea offered black with neither sugar nor cream); "goin' down the road" (leaving Atlantic Canada to look for work); and the ubiquitous "my son" (offered as a friendly greeting between males of any age regardless of familial bonds or age difference).

Psychedelic

This is another one of those things I'm surprised isn't more widely known: the word "psychedelic" was coined by Weyburn, Saskatchewan, psychiatrist Humphrey Osmond. Really? Weyburn? Saskatchewan? Humphrey? *Psy-che-freaking-delic!*

Sacres

These awesomely colourful French Canadian curses reference the Roman Catholic church and often appear as stereotypes of Québecers in popular culture. Some examples are: *Sacrebleu! Sacrement!* and the ever popular *Tabernacle!* (pronounced "tab-arr-NAK").

Sorry

Canadians are infamous for saying "Sorry" at awesomely inappropriate times, such as when jostled in the street or when their toes are trodden on. Instead of quizzically or angrily expanding the acronym "WTF?" to its uncondensed state, Canadians, even when *they* are the wronged parties, are likely to reflexively blurt out, "Sorry!"

Thank You

If we say "Sorry" at inappropriate times, we *always* say "Thank you," whether it is warranted or not. We are famous for this (apparently). Please don't thank me for pointing this out. Sorry if that hurt your feelings, eh?

Two-four

Slang for a carton of 24 beers. "Two-four" has also appropriately bled into an alternate way of referring to Victoria Day, the May long weekend (associated with heavy alcohol consumption, as are most long weekends in Canada) also known as the May Two-four weekend.

GROUPS AND EVENTS

There is much that is awesome in Canadian history. As with all the awesomeness in this book, most of Canada's historical facts are tough to categorize appropriately. For example, while Vikings are undoubtedly awesome, should they be in the category of "Awesome People" (which they undoubtedly were) or in the category of "Horned-Hat-Wearing Berserkers of Scandinavian Heritage," which is only partly accurate and runs the risk of being a category that consists of only one item. Similarly, the Battle of the Plains of Abraham was definitely an event, as was the On to Ottawa Trek. However, the former lasted approximately 12 minutes, while the latter went on for several weeks. What to do? You may judge for yourself as to the fitness of the categories that follow. Please direct all corre-spondence, inquiries and letters of outrage to the publisher.

Vikings

Most modern nations up and down the eastern coasts of the Americas can claim Spanish, French or English explorers as their conquering founders. Not Canada. The first Europeans to land in this country were Vikings, who settled a small community at L'Anse aux Meadows around 1000 AD.

The Fur Trade

From the early 1600s to the early 1800s, the soon-to-be nation of Canada was shaped by the fur trade. Fraught with romance, adventure and wealth, the fur trade helped form both Canada and its perception in the eyes of the rest of the world as a place where fortunes could be made and wild romance had.

Filles du roi

Between 1665 and 1673, nearly 800 "King's Daughters" were shipped from France to Québec for the express purpose of marrying the hardy settlers of New France. There is no truth to the notion that they were prostitutes; rather, they were a mixture of rural and urban unfortunates who helped to weave the fabric of a new nation.

Coureurs de bois

Known in English as "runners of the woods," these fur-trading frontiersmen and trappers were the backbone of the fur trade and, in turn, of Canada's early economy. Although heavily romanticized by the lens of history, theirs was probably a life of hardship interspersed with periods of prosperity.

Hommes du nord

These "men of the North" were the voyageurs who paddled all through the winter months and were the embodiment of the romantic image of voyageurs as tough, joyous mercenaries capable of superhuman exertion. They were also known as the *l'hivernants,* or "winterers."

Mangeurs de lard

These less-hardy brethren of *les hommes du nord* (see above) paddled only easy routes that did not become as cold during winter months. Regarded as sissies in the voyageur realm, they ate a steady diet of salt pork and so earned themselves the French nickname *mangeurs de lard*, or "eaters of pork."

Plains of Abraham

The Battle of the Plains of Abraham, which took place on September 13, 1759, is widely regarded as the first tumbling domino in the sequence of events that led to the collapse of French dominance in Canada. Once the firing began in Québec City, the battle between the French and English armies may have been over in as little as 12 minutes. It was an awesome outcome for the British, who really ought not to have expected their outrageously risky plan to succeed.

Mounties

Short for Royal Canadian Mounted Police (RCMP), the Mounties, in their tunics of scarlet serge, are an awesomely visible presence at important events and ceremonies, as well as an awesomely invisible presence as they set about keeping the nation safe with their undercover work. If you believe a certain outmoded stereotypical view of Canada, *all of us* are red-jacketed Mounties, riding our dogsleds home to our igloos after a long day of fur trapping and pitching wholesome woo to our French Canadian sweethearts.

Gold Rush

Besides the obvious appeal of large amounts of gold, the inherent awesomeness of the gold rush in shaping Canada's character was the potential not just to get rich but to get rich quick. The frontier gold-rush towns that sprang up were as close as Canada got to the individualistic outlook of the U.S. Wild West.

Charlottetown Conference

The 1864 conference that paved the way for Confederation could have ended much differently. Originally, it was only intended to explore the possibility of a union of the Maritime provinces, but a contingent of Canadians who showed up as "observers" pitched a union of *all* the provinces, which would eventually become Canada. The Slaymaker and Nichol's Circus was in Charlottetown at the same time, stealing all the thunder and using up all the city's hotel rooms. Furthermore, the Canadian "observers" had arrived in a yacht with a well-stocked wine cellar. The Charlottetown Conference is an awesome example of one nation's history founded in happenstance, booze and performing dogs.

On to Ottawa

This 1935 railway trek to Ottawa by unemployed men from all across Canada set the stage for the many welfare and work reforms that followed the Depression era. The phrase itself still lingers in Canada's social argot as an echo of the working poor demanding help.

INVENTIONS

Canadians are, by their very natures, inventive. Perhaps it comes from living in an environment where building houses out of blocks of snow is not merely an option, but for generations was the only option. Imagine then, what we can do when given a laboratory and a dog pancreas, or a decaying isotope or a roomful of medical students. Here you will find both the inventions and the inventors who invented them (to paraphrase one of my favourite redundant sentences). And let me finish by saying that, no, the zipper is not included, because it was not invented by a Canadian. It was invented by a Swedish American who happened to manufacture it at one of his Canadian plants. Dissent is neither encouraged nor tolerated. In short, if you disagree, you can zip it.

Insulin

Famously isolated and extracted by Frederick Banting and Charles Best at the University of Toronto in 1921, daily insulin shots have saved, prolonged and improved the lives of countless diabetics since.

Pablum

The world's first "instant" baby food was invented in 1930 at Toronto's Hospital for Sick Children to battle malnutrition in infants, which can lead to rickets, among other disorders. Three resident doctors, Alan Brown, Fred Tisdale and Theo Drake, are to thank.

Time Zones

Among his many other *awesomenesses*, Sir Sandford Fleming (see p. 85) championed and helped to implement the standardization of time zones, which is one reason that everything occurs a half-hour later in Newfoundland.

Pacemaker

Cardiac medicine took a major step forward in 1951 with the development of the world's first external pacemaker at the University of Toronto, led by Dr. John Hopps.

WonderBra

The WonderBra, in the first of its many incarnations, was co-developed by American Israeli Pilot and Montréaler Moe Nadler, with Nadler later acquiring all the rights. By the mid-1960s, WonderBra was beginning to position itself as a brand that was comfortable, practical and sexy, the image of WonderBra that many people hold today.

Bone Marrow Transplant Therapy

Although no one person can be said to have "invented" bone marrow transplant therapy for cancer patients, doctors James Till of Lloydminster and Ernest McCulloch of Toronto made a huge contribution to this field when they demonstrated the existence of stem cells in 1963.

Buckley's Mixture

The infamous cough syrup advertised since 1986 by the unforgettable slogan, "It tastes awful. And it works." was invented in 1920 by Toronto pharmacist W.K. Buckley. His son Frank became the company's spokesperson for the famous series of "It tastes awful." TV commercials.

Perimeter Institute

Housed in Waterloo, Ontario, the Perimeter Institute's noble goal is a greater understanding of the nature of the universe with special attention to quantum physics and theory. If there is a parallel you, reading a parallel book in a parallel universe the Perimeter Institute may be among the first organizations to let the both of you know about it.

INVENTORS AND INNOVATORS

Sir Sandford Fleming (1827–1915)

Fleming was a man of immense energy, intelligence and curiosity. As well as championing and refining the notion of standard time, he was also the chief engineer and surveyor for the construction of the Canadian Pacific Railway and became a leading advocate for the first transatlantic telegraph cable. He was a founding member of both the Royal Society of Canada and the Royal Canadian Institute. And if all this weren't enough, as an avid sketcher, Fleming also designed Canada's first postage stamp in 1851.

Sir William Osler (1849–1919)

If you've ever wondered why you hear so much about this Canadian physician, it's only because he pretty much single-handedly invented the medical residency model that sees doctors learning at the bedside of patients rather than just in the lecture hall. He also recommended that doctors listen carefully to patients and take detailed patient histories. As well as writing and publishing prolifically, he was also an inveterate practical joker, often writing ridiculous letters to newspapers under the name of "Egerton Yorrick Davis."

Reginald Aubrey Fessenden (1866–1932)

Fessenden held hundreds of patents relating to radio broadcasting and is widely recognized as a brilliant technician and inventor. However, he is best known for what is regarded as likely the first-ever transmission of music via radio waves. The demonstration took place on Christmas Eve 1906, when ships at sea were startled to hear first the music of Handel and later violin music played by Fessenden himself, both sounds coming through the equipment normally used for transmitting Morse code.

Peter Lymburner Robertson (1879–1951)

After cutting his hand when a flat-head screw driver slipped off the screw head, Robertson invented the square-socket screw that bears his name. A commercial success in Canada, Robertson screws never really took off in the U.S., probably, in part, because Robertson refused to issue a licence to Henry Ford so Ford could use Robertson screws in his U.S. auto production lines.

Wilder Penfield (1891–1976)

An imaginative and, some would say, unorthodox neurosurgeon, Penfield is renowned for electrically stimulating the brains of conscious patients to observe their responses and better map the brain's functions. Penfield also developed a successful treatment for epilepsy that involved destroying the affected brain cells.

Carl Agar (1901–68)

If you were to boil down Agar's most memorable contribution to aviation to a single sentence that he may or may not have ever uttered, it would be, "Of course you can land a helicopter on a mountain." Agar pioneered the use of helicopters at high altitudes and as delivery vessels for construction supplies and other large, heavy items that needed to be delivered to otherwise inaccessible areas.

James Gosling (b. 1955)

Born in Alberta, Gosling invented the Java programming language in 1994. Among its many other useful functions, Java helps websites with video and audio to run smoothly and quickly. Gosling was made an officer of the Order of Canada in 2007.

Sylvia Fedoruk (1927–2012)

This remarkable woman was best known for three things: being key to the development of the first Cobalt-60 unit, useful for medical imaging and treatment of some forms of cancer; being the 17th lieutenant-governor of Saskatchewan; and for being a champion...curler! It's also worth mentioning that she was the first woman to become a member of the Atomic Energy Control Board of Canada and the first female Chancellor of the University of Saskatchewan.

NAME THAT TUNESMITH

*Yes, yes, yes—an entire book could be written about the
Canadian music scene (and indeed there are many), but
because of space considerations, we've opted to simply pay
tribute to a few of our most awesome singers, musicians and
composers. You will find more of them in the "Pretty Cool"
section near the end of this book, but do not take offence if you
find someone there you consider to be "awesome"—it's the
thought that counts.*

Paul Anka (b. 1941)

The prototypical teen heartthrob, Anka sprang out of the
Ottawa suburbs to record a string of hits while in his mid-teens.
He appeared in film, toured with the stars and continues to enthral
audiences today.

Arcade Fire

More or less commencing activity in 2001, this American-Canadian
hybrid band has a unique, sometimes sad sound. They won the
2011 Grammy Award for Album of the Year for *The Suburbs*.

Jann Arden (b. 1962)

Singer, songwriter, talk-show host, sometime restaurateur and
all-round good egg, Jann Arden is the awesomely approachable
writer of the hit song, "Insensitive."

The Band

First taking the name "The Band" in 1970, this group of
multi-instrumentalist Canadians and Americans helped to forge
the tradition that would eventually morph into "country-rock,"

with instrumentation and arrangements going far beyond the traditional four-piece rock band.

Barenaked Ladies

Formed in 1988 in Scarborough, Ontario, "BNL," as they have come to be called, were the kings of the early 1990s quirky alt-rock, before outlasting nearly all of the contemporaries to become a veritable Canadian institution.

Justin Bieber (b. 1994)

Love him or hate him, you can't deny the worldwide success of this kid from Stratford, Ontario, who has shifted millions upon millions of units, caused veritable palpitations in pubescent hearts the world over and whose every change in hairstyle makes headlines.

Broken Social Scene

Becoming active around 1999, this group seems like a truly Canadian notion: a "musical collective" with revolving membership consisting of the cream of the cream of Canada's *other* top rock acts.

Leonard Cohen (b. 1934)

Since the 1960s, Cohen has been known as Canada's prolific and wholly unique melancholic troubadour, singing many of his classic songs in a sad, droning manner, while somehow still scoring far and wide with women.

Celine Dion (b. 1968)

This French Canadian chanteuse/belter extraordinaire was a teen star in Québec, later rising to such rarefied heights of global stardom that she has gone into residency in Las Vegas. She is estimated to have sold 200 million records worldwide.

Drake (b. 1986)

Aubrey Drake Graham started his career playing Jimmy Brooks on *Degrassi: The Next Generation*, from 2001 to 2009. Then he transformed himself into the chart-topping rapper, Drake, and has never looked back.

Glenn Gould (1932–82)

Recognized as Canada's foremost classical pianist and interpreter of Bach, Gould was also a prolific writer, musical theorist and eagerly embraced new technology. He also played a charmingly eccentric array of characters in TV reviews and other appearances.

The Guess Who

This 1970s AM-radio staple needs no introduction, charting hits such as "American Woman," "Share the Land" and "These Eyes."

Sarah Harmer (b. 1970)

This tuneful, socially conscious singer, songwriter and musician is also notable for being an outspoken and effective environmental crusader.

Jeff Healey (1966–2008)

This blind guitarist played sitting down with his guitar on his lap, unleashing some of the most ferocious and joyful rock-blues ever to emerge from north of the 49th parallel. He was also a musicologist, radio host and trad-jazz aficionado, playing trumpet with various jazz bands.

K'naan (b. 1978)

Born in Somalia, K'naan settled in Rexdale, Ontario, when his family moved to Canada. Learning English and rap diction from listening to hip-hop recordings, K'naan had set the stage for his rise to prominence in the mid-2000s, culminating with the choice of his song, "Wavin' Flag," as Coca-Cola's theme for the 2010 FIFA World Cup.

Kardinall Official (b. 1976)

Lauded as Canada's "hip-hop Ambassador," he is one of Canada's top hip-hop producers and, in his 2001 hit, "BaKardi Slang," popularized "T Dot" as a nickname for Toronto.

Anton Kuerti (b. 1938)

Born in Austria, Kuerti is a prolific classical pianist and the founder of the Festival of the Sound in Parry Sound, Ontario. He performs all across Canada and is often heard on CBC Radio.

k.d. lang (b. 1961)

After bursting onto the Canadian music scene in the 1980s with a country-rockabilly sensibility, k.d. lang of Alberta quickly emerged as a diverse singer-songwriter with a lush, creamy voice and remarkably pure tone. She is also well known as an exponent of gay rights.

Avril Lavigne (b. 1984)

Arguably Canada's first mainstream "riotgrrl," Napanee, Ontario's Lavigne rose to prominence with her hit "Sk8er Boi," launching a career of no-nonsense, straight-ahead, attitudinal rock.

Metric

Although formed in 1998, Metric can certainly be called a band of the "new millennium" with a long catalogue of hummable, hard-edged, contemporary rock songs.

Joni Mitchell (b. 1943)

She is one of Canada's earliest and foremost singers, songwriters and composers in the folk-rock genre. Coming to prominence in the late 1960s and early 1970s, her name is recognized the world over.

Alanis Morissette (b. 1974)

After early success as a big-haired teen popster, Morissette went on to a tsunami of worldwide success with *Jagged Little Pill* (1995), a defiant portrait of anger, confidence, insecurity and, against all odds, occasionally finding love.

Anne Murray (b. 1945)

Famous for her amazingly pure tone and full voice, Murray was the first Canadian female solo artist to have a U.S. number one song with "Snowbird" (1970). Decades of success both at home and abroad followed.

Oscar Peterson (1925–2007)

A jazz pianist of world renown and immense ability, Peterson was also known as a generous musician whose playing often left room for collaborators to take the spotlight.

Paul Robeson (1898–1976)

Robeson was an African American actor and singer and political activist who had his passport revoked in the 1950s because of his belief that communism was not necessarily inherently bad and also for suggesting that the U.S. government was guilty of genocide for failing to prevent countless lynchings in the Deep South. Invited to give a concert in Canada but unable to travel without a valid passport, Robeson and his supporters found a unique solution. On May 18, 1952, Robeson drove to the Peace Arch on the border of Washington State and BC. There, from the back of a flat-bed truck, he sang a heartfelt concert for a mixed crowed of 40,000 Americans and Canadians, each standing on their respective sides of the border. It was a defiant *F*ck You* to the U.S. government.

Rush

Formed in 1969 but not achieving its current line-up until 1974, this iconically Canadian three-piece band (Geddy Lee, Alex Lifeson, Neil Peart) is known for its complex and sometimes multi-tasking musicianship, eclectic lyrical composition and for generally being regarded as prog-rock gods by at least two generations of kids from the suburbs.

Buffy Sainte-Marie (b. 1941)

This Cree singer, songwriter and activist is a Canadian legend. Much of her work focused on indigenous peoples, and she also appeared regularly on *Sesame Street* in the 1970s (famously breast-feeding her infant son in one episode). She penned the Academy Award–winning song "Up Where We Belong" for the 1982 film *An Officer and a Gentleman*.

Paul Schaffer (b. 1942)

For several years, Paul Schaffer seemed to be everywhere, popping up as musical director at countless high-profile concerts and events. First rising to prominence as a regular member the of *Saturday Night Live* house band, since 1982, he has been David Letterman's bandleader and de facto co-host.

Stompin' Tom Connors (1936–2013)

Proof of his awesomeness: authorship of "Bud the Spud," "Big Joe Mufferaw," "Sudbury Saturday Night" and "The Hockey Song." Bonus awesomeness: he boycotted the 1978 (and returned his six) Juno Awards because they were given out to Canadians who no longer resided in this country. Conclusive awesomeness: a proud Canadian who stood by his convictions. After he died family, friends and fans held a raucous memorial planned by Tom himself at the Peterborough Memorial Centre. Fans came from across the country to attend.

The Tragically Hip

Formed in 1983, "the Hip" have eased into their status as elders of contemporary Canadian rock. Their long list of Canadian-flavoured hits includes "New Orleans is Sinking," "Ahead by a Century," "Fireworks" and "Bobcaygeon," to name just a few.

Shania Twain (b. 1965)

From a childhood of poverty in Timmins, Ontario, Twain sang her way to stardom, starting in bars and roadhouses, and eventually rising to worldwide superstardom.

Neil Young (b. 1945)

Called by some the "Godfather of Grunge," Young's career as a rock guitarist, singer and composer likely need no introduction. He has found success as a solo artist, as part of Buffalo Springfield and Crosby, Stills, Nash and Young, as well as with frequent collaborators, Crazy Horse.

FORTITUDE OR MADNESS?

Once, on a lecture tour of England, the noted Canadian economist and humorist Stephen Leacock recounted this introduction by a well-meaning vicar:

"Not so long ago, ladies and gentlemen," said the vicar, "we used to send out to Canada various classes of our community to help build up that country. We sent out our labourers, we sent out our scholars and professors. Indeed we even sent out our criminals. And now," with a wave of his hand towards me, "they are coming back."

While it's a popular notion among Canadians that we are all descended from tough coureurs de bois *and sexy* filles du roi, *the reality is that the people who discovered, explored and settled our fair land were a much more diverse lot than that. I present a small slice of the awesome truth.*

Madeleine Jarret Tarieu (1678–1747)

In 1692, 14-year-old Madeleine lived with her parents at Fort Verchères in Québec. One day, when most of the able-bodied adults were away, the local Iroquois attacked (quite rightly wanting to get their land back). In a strike for the Europeans, though, Madeleine dashed inside the fort and fired the cannon, scaring off the invaders. This is all we know with any certainty. The rest of the tale has been embroidered and expanded with numerous details now impossible to confirm or disprove.

Isobel Gunn (c. 1780–1861)

Credited by the Hudson's Bay Company as its "first female adventurer," Isobel Gunn disguised herself as a man ("John Fubbister") and signed on to a 2900-kilometre voyage with the company. The journey culminated in 1807 when Gunn's cover was blown by the small matter of her giving birth to a baby boy at an HBC fort in Pembina in present-day North Dakota. HBC honoured the remainder of her contract, but she was relegated to "woman's work," cooking and cleaning. In 1809, she and her son were shipped back to Scotland's Orkney Islands, from whence they had come.

Sir John Franklin (1786–1847)

Until frozen corpses from his final expedition began to be unearthed in the 1980s, no one knew what had become of British explorer Sir John Franklin. A theatrical aura of mystery and tragedy surrounds the demise of this awesomely incompetent and inflexible man. Exploring a new and hostile land is never easy, but in an awesomely barmy decision-making process, Franklin was given additional commands after his first expedition to Canada lost 11 out of 22 men (some to cannibalism, no less).

Mina Benson Hubbard (1870–1956)

After her husband died in a 1903 expedition to map parts of Labrador, Mina set out to avenge his memory after his travelling companion wrote an unflattering book about the experience. She outfitted and commanded a small expedition that travelled nearly 1000 kilometres in 1905, exploring and mapping the terrain her husband had never gotten to see. Overtaking a rival expedition mounted by her husband's detractor, she exonerated his name and penned her own book, *A Woman's Way Through Unknown Labrador*.

ONE OF A KIND

Many people equate the word "heritage" with "history," but I prefer to think of heritage also as something that we share. The varied and manifold awesomeness that follows is unarguably shared by all Canadians. We can visit, gawk, appreciate and experience the many wonders outlined in this section. From the large to the small, from the majestic to the utterly silly, from the noble to the foolish—awesomeness of all stripes makes its home in Canada.

Yukon

As if the nearly pristine state of this territory's scenery isn't awesome enough, there are all the awesome festivals, many of which echo the gold rush history of the area.

Northwest Territories

Besides the territory's ghost towns, many active mines, stunning scenery, long daylight hours and exceptional opportunities to see the northern lights, the awesome Legislative Assembly building looks like a flying saucer in the middle of a thicket of trees.

Nunavut

Canada's newest territory (formed in 1999) has an inukshuk on its flag and a caribou and a narwhal on its coat of arms. That, right there, is already seriously awesome. Nunavut is the size of western Europe and has the midnight sun and the coldest weather of anywhere in Canada. *Chimo.*

British Columbia

It's hard not to start with the spectacular mountain ranges: Coast, Columbia and Rocky. There are also the various First Nations influences, Haida Gwaii islands and the beautiful cities. The better you know it, the more awesome BC is.

Alberta

Let's see…the Rocky Mountains, the Oil Patch, the Calgary Stampede, Banff National Park, amazing dinosaur fossils, grain fields, beekeeping (Really? Beekeeping?) and Lake Louise. It doesn't get much *awesomer.*

Saskatchewan

The province is almost perfectly rectangular in shape, it eschews daylight savings time, our health-care system was born there, it has canola, potash, forestry, Saskatoon berries and Moose Jaw is rightly called "The Friendly City." Anyone for awesome?

Manitoba

Frankly, any province or territory that has polar bears doesn't need much more awesomeness, but Manitoba also has particularly good northern lights viewing, the "world's windiest" intersection at Portage and Main and it's the place where the infamous Winnipeg General Strike of 1919 took place.

Ontario

The federal capital is located in Ontario, but I recognize that not everyone thinks that's awesome. Okay, well, there's also the amazing scenery, the CN Tower, Algonquin Park, the Great Lakes, the St. Lawrence Seaway, all that agriculture and a fair amount of touristy stuff.

Québec

Old Montréal alone counts for all kinds of awesome in my book (and this is my book), but then there's Québec City, poutine, subsidized daycare, a vibrant Francophone culture separate from the rest of Canada, Schwartz's deli, the Québec film industry and Carnaval.

New Brunswick

The awesomeness starts with the name. How many other provinces are named after the ancestral German home of an English king? The heart of Acadian culture is in New Brunswick, it has the Reversing Falls and St. John is the oldest incorporated city in Canada.

Prince Edward Island

To start with, it's the only province that's an island, which is pretty awesome, but it also has bright red mud, is arguably the potato capital of Canada, Anne of Green Gables was created there and PEI is the birthplace of Confederation.

Nova Scotia

Atlantic awesomeness gets a workout with rich and accessible history, the city of Halifax, Peggy's Cove, the oldest blockhouse in North America at Fort Edward and, in typically progressive Canadian fashion, the largest black settlement in North America was at Birchtown.

Newfoundland and Labrador

How are thee awesome? Let me count the ways. Newfoundland English's rich and distinct culture within Anglo Canada, the province's breathtaking scenery, all the great seafood and local dishes, Maritime lifestyle in general and the super-friendly people.

AWESOME UNDERTAKINGS

Canadian Pacific Railway

Built from 1881 to 1885, this titanic undertaking helped to forge the nation and gave us such famous names as Kicking Horse Pass and Rogers Pass.

CPR Hotels

The CPR wasn't just busy building a railway; they were also busy building massive and magnificent hotels for their travellers. Soon, monumental hotels arose like oases of comfort that were out of place but at home amid the wilds of Canada.

Trent-Severn Waterway

Awesomely useless to industry but good for small pleasure craft, this waterway in Ontario was built piecemeal between 1833 and 1920. It comprises 45 locks and stretches for 387 kilometres.

RC Harris Water Purification Plant

After taking nine years to build, when the plant opened in 1941 it was dubbed the "palace of purification" for its opulent, sprawling art deco design. Looking like Hollywood's version of a super villain's stronghold, it has appeared in countless films while it continues to provide 45 percent of Toronto's potable water.

St. Lawrence Seaway

When it opened in 1959, the St. Lawrence Seaway was recognized as a major feat of engineering, allowing ships to travel from the Atlantic Ocean to the Great Lakes by passing through a system of locks that gradually elevates the ships between 75 and 99 metres!

Gardiner Dam, Saskatchewan

The world's largest earth-filled dam is 5 kilometres long, 64 metres high, took eight years to build (1959–67) and used 65-million cubic metres of dirt!

TransCanada Highway

It may seem odd to describe a highway as awesome, but if you've ever driven across Canada, you can more easily understand some people's connection to what is, after all, a squiggly ribbon of asphalt that happens to be 8000 kilometres long.

The 401

Not that it's unique but, if you find yourself driving through southern Ontario and want to avoid Toronto (and really, who doesn't) then the famed 401 is your best bet, acting like a hyper-space route across the top of the city and enabling speedy travel (assuming traffic is not congested).

Vancouver Central Library

Covering an entire city block and including an office tower, the central branch of the Vancouver Library is an awesome collage of architectural styles and forms.

THEY REALLY DID THAT?

West Edmonton Mall

Until 2004, Alberta's West Edmonton Mall was the world's largest indoor shopping mall (at 5.3 million square feet)—now it is merely the largest in North America. Its awesome attractions include a roller coaster, an artificial lake, a skating rink, a water park, a saltwater habitat and a miniature golf course. The mall is also accredited as a zoo. What? No indoor ski hill?

Sukanen Ship Pioneer Village and Museum

In the late 1930s, Finnish-born prairie farmer Tom Sukanen set about building his own boat to return to his homeland. The only problem was that he built his boat in landlocked Saskatchewan. Although most of the vessel was completed, Sukanen had trouble finding anywhere to launch it. Decades later, its hulk became the centrepiece of a no-less-than-outrageous undertaking—a *building* museum. Starting in the 1970s, old houses and other structures were painstakingly moved from all across Saskatchewan to form a museum that feels more like a little town, complete with a grain elevator!

Regina

While many things are awesome about Regina, what I'm referring to is the sheer audacity of humankind to plonk a patch of itself down in the middle of a howling prairie. Seriously, drive into Regina from somewhere like Moose Jaw, and what you'll see coming off the highway is flat, flat, flat, Regina, flat, flat, flat. It's just *there*.

Cochin Lighthouse

Although Saskatchewan doesn't exactly have easy access to any oceans, it has many, many lakes and on a slender isthmus between Cochin Lake and Jackfish Lake is the province's *only* lighthouse.

Churchill

Aside from being the so-called "Polar Bear Capital of the World" and a great place to see Beluga whales or northern lights, Churchill, Manitoba, is Canada's only arctic seaport.

Diefenbunkers

These cavernous underground nuclear fallout shelters were built in the late 1950s and early '60s and disparagingly named after then prime minister John Diefenbaker. You can visit the last remaining Diefenbunker in Carp, Ontario.

Flin Flon

From 2002 to 2009, this unusually named Manitoba community was also the site of Canada's (at that time) only government-approved marijuana mine…er, rather, *legally sanctioned* grow-op in the bottom of an old copper mine (for medicinal purposes and all that).

The Lost Villages of Ontario

In the closing years of the 1950s, the route of the proposed St. Lawrence Seaway passed through several small villages and towns. After extensive planning and relocation of the residents to new communities, on July 1, 1958, the areas were all flooded, their structures submerged forever beneath the waves. Nowadays, the lost villages make for awesome scuba diving.

Casa Loma

At one time the largest private residence in Canada, this castle-like mansion in Toronto has stables, awesomely carved wooden panelling and, best of all, secret passages! And during World War II, it was converted into a secret facility for building sonar sensors to detect enemy submarines. Awesome accomplished.

Fathom Five National Marine Park

Located in southern Ontario's Georgian Bay, Canada's first marine conservation area is essentially Disneyland for scuba divers, featuring 22 shipwrecks, 7500-year-old trees and the remains of a former waterfall. Its catchy Shakespearean name doesn't hurt either.

Hôtel de Glace

Designed anew every December, the Ice Hotel in Québec City is open for business each January. As its name succinctly suggests, the hotel is made entirely out of ice—360 tonnes of it to be exact. There is a bar, a dance floor and a chapel for weddings (insert your own frigidity joke here).

AWESOMELY ALIVE (OR DEAD) HISTORY

Ksan Village

At this re-creation of an 1870s settlement of the Gitxsan First Nation of BC, you can visit traditional longhouses, as well as the carving school, where young woodcarvers learn the age-old skills of their forebears.

Kwäday Dän Ts'inchi

Meaning "long-ago person found," this was the name given to a naturally mummified 500-year-old male youth discovered in 1999, emerging from a glacier in BC's Tatshenshini-Alsek park. Although his head and some of his limbs were missing, Dän's intact stomach yielded the information that he had been eating quite well, including wild asparagus, salmon, deer meat and berries. His cause of death remains unknown, but his last few meals have been recorded for the ages. Through DNA testing with two local First Nations bands, 17 living people were found who are related to Dän on his mother's side.

Inukshuks

Likely created to mark migratory routes of caribou in a landscape otherwise devoid of landmarks, these sometimes human-shaped cairns of stones have become a friendly Canadian icon. An inukshuk was the logo of the 2010 Winter Olympics in Vancouver, and miniature ones can be found in tacky souvenir shops all across the land.

Igloos

Although not needed nearly as often as they once were, the skills needed to build a house out of snow are still handed down from generation to generation in some families, keeping alive the knowledge of centuries past.

Grain Elevators

Also called the "Sentinels of the Prairies," there were once nearly 6000 of these friendly wooden towers scattered in clusters across the prairies. Now just two "elevator rows" are left, in Inglis, Manitoba, and Warner, Alberta, where you can see old-fashioned grouped grain elevators as they once appeared over the prairies.

Québec City

Canada's oldest capital city offers an awesome mix of history and modernity with buildings hundreds of years old nestled comfortably alongside glass high-rises.

Halifax

Besides an amazing range of functional architecture ranging from the 1800s forward, Nova Scotia's capital city also has an awesome selection of beautiful, tiny apartment buildings ranging from the mid-20th century.

GIANT THINGS

Canadian communities like to have the "World's Biggest" things, but for some reason, this predilection seems to be intensified on the Prairies. Awesomely big, here are just some of the large objects you will find improbably erected all across the Prairies in the hope that they will serve as roadside attractions. Remember, everything on this list is giant, and I'm counting them all as one awesome thing, so you can't say you didn't get good value for your money.

Alberta

Badminton Racket (St. Albert)

Baseball Bat (Wainwright)

Battling Bear and Swan (Swan Hills)

Beaver (Beaverlodge)

Blue Heron (Barrhead)

Bucking Bronco and Rider (Ponoka)

Chuckwagon (Dewberry)

Cowboy Boot (Edmonton)

Dinosaur (Drumheller)

Dragonfly (Wabamun)

Geese (Hanna)

Gopher (Torrington)

Horse (Irricana)

Kubasa (Mundare)

Mallard Duck (Andrew)

Mushroom (Vilna)

Oil Derrick (Redwater)

Oil Lamp (Donalda)

Painting on Easel (Altona)

Perogy (Glendon)

Piggy Bank (Coleman)

Pumpkin (Smoky Lake)

Putter (Bow Island)

Softball (Chauvin)

Sundial (Lloydminster)

Tallest Teepee (Medicine Hat)

Ukrainian Easter Egg, or *Pysanka* (Vegreville)

USS *Enterprise* (Vulcan)

Saskatchewan

Avocet, Plover (Chaplin)

Bunnock (Macklin)

Burrowing Owls, Sturgeon, Ord's Kangaroo Rats, Meadowlark, Prairie Rattlesnake, Ferruginous Hawk (Leader)

Candle (Candle Lake)

Chokecherry Cluster (Lancer)

Coffee Percolator and Cup (Davidson)

Diefenbaker Stamp (Humboldt)

Gopher (Eston)

Grasshopper (Wilkie)

Guitars (Craven and Cut Knife)

Hockey Cards (Kelvington)

Honeybee (Tisdale)

Letter "G" (Grayson)

Lily, Sunflower (Balcarres)

Moose (Moose Jaw)

Oil Can, Diamond, Baseball Cap (Rocanville)

Plesiosaur (Ponteix)

Saber-toothed Tiger (Martinsville)

Santa Claus (Watson)

Snowflake (Wawota)

Still (Vonda)

Tomahawk (Cut Knife)

Turtle (Turtleford)

Ukrainian Maiden (Canora)

Wheat (Rosthern)

Woolly Mammoth (Kyle)

Manitoba

1931 Rolls Royce (Steinbach)

Bear, Purple Martin Colony, Turtle (Boissevain)

Bull (Russell)

Camel (Glenboro)

Canada Goose (Lundar)

Canvasback Duck (Minnedosa)

Catfish (Selkirk)

Curling Rock (Arborg)

Eagle, Grey Owl, Windmill, Coke Can (Portage la Prairie)

Elk (Onanole)

Fire Hydrant (Elm Creek)

Garter Snakes (Inwood)

Happy Rock (Gladstone)

Heron (Langruth)

Holstein Cow (La Broquerie)

Inukshuk, Polar Bears (Churchill)

Jewel (Roblin)

Lourdes Grotto Replica (Ste. Rose du Lac)

Mallard Duck (Petersfield)

Mosquito (Komarno)

Mushrooms (Meleb)

Pumpkin (Roland)

Rose (Inglis)

Rose (Sandy Lake)

Sharptail Grouse (Ashern)

Smoking Pipe (Saint Claude)

Snow Goose (Dunrea)

Sturgeon (Dominion City)

Sundial (Pinawa)

Swan (Swan River)

Viking (Gimli)

Viking Ship (Erickson)

White Horse (St. Francois Xavier)

Wild Turkey (La Riviere)

The Prairies do not have a monopoly on big things, but I recognize that your curiosity in that subject may now be sated, so briefly, some others are:

The Big Nickel (Sudbury, Ontario)

Canada Goose (Wawa, Ontario)

Giant Axe (Nackawic, New Brunswick)

Giant Lobster (Shediac, New Brunswick)

AWESOME FORTIFICATIONS

Fort Calgary Historic Park

This reconstruction of a mid-to-late 19th-century North West Mounted Police fortification gives visitors a true sense of how spartan life could be in the early days of the Prairies. Originally built to discourage whiskey traders, Fort Calgary is now a proud reminder of rougher days.

Fort York

There aren't many places in Toronto where you can hear a noon-day gun (insert your own urban crime joke here). But if you live close to Fort York, you can almost set your watch by the mid-day cannon blast. Well, okay, you can't set your watch by it, because it happens between 12:30 PM and 1:00 PM on a pretty elastic schedule, actually. Oh, and the red-jacketed re-enactors only fire the cannon off between Canada Day and Labour Day. But still, living as I do within earshot of it, the cannon's blast always heartens me.

La Citadelle

In many ways, Québec City's Citadelle is emblematic of Canada itself—the French began its construction, and the British finished it (to fortify Québec against an American attack that never came). All the more amazing is that, with some sections clocking in at more than 200 years old, la Citadelle is still a functioning military barracks, home to the famous Van Doos regiment.

Fortifications de Québec

By the time the 1850s rolled around, the venerable worthies of Québec City realized that they no longer needed the 90-year-old ramparts that surrounded the city. So they cleverly opened up the ramparts to foot traffic, allowing sightseers to walk around the perimeter on top of the massive fortifications, surveying the domain and bestriding the world like collossi.

Fortress Louisberg

This awesomely detailed national historic site is a painstakingly accurate reconstruction of what life inside the fortress walls was like in the 1740s. You can find re-enactors portraying every aspect of 18th-century life in Nova Scotia—labourers, merchants and fishmongers—not just hoity-toity, gold-tasselled military personnel.

The Citadel

Perched majestically and yet still somehow cheerily atop a hill that overlooks Halifax, the Citadel dates from 1856. Part of its awesomeness today stems from the men in kilts who stage twice-daily musket drills.

NORTHERN GRANDEUR

Well, this is it—the beginning of the section you knew I had to include—Canada's (many)[10] awesome natural sites and phenomena. See how I put "many" in brackets and then to the power of 10? That's because Canada has so much natural awesomeness that I needed to save space (instead of writing "many" 10 times in a row), space that I filled up with this explanation of how I saved space, thereby not saving any space at all. Perhaps cutting to the awesomely natural chase is what I had better do.

Eskers

These long, winding ridges of sand and gravel found across Canada are thought to follow the paths of glacial streams during the melt of the last ice age. The Thelon Esker runs for the 800 kilometres between the Northwest Territories and Nunavut, while the Munro Esker in Ontario is 250 kilometres long and nearly 50 kilometres wide.

Baffin Island

Mountains, fjords, polar bears, kayaking, sparse population, the Arctic Circle—if chilly, rugged scenery is your thing, Baffin Island is the place for you.

BC Waterfalls

BC has Canada's four highest waterfalls: Della Falls, Takakkaw Falls, Hunlen Falls and Helmcken Falls, each with its own awesomely spectacular surroundings.

Haida Gwaii

Formerly known as the Queen Charlotte Islands, this West Coast archipelago has a unique ecosystem that dates from before the last ice age. It is also the traditional home of the Haida First Nation, as well as being the world's only source of "black slate" argillite.

Athabasca Falls

Alberta's most famous waterfall is an awesome sight to be seen and an awesome sound to be heard. Take a raincoat.

Lake Louise

The breathtaking scenery of this Alberta mountain lake's famously turquoise waters is the main attraction, but nearby is Canada's highest community (of the same name) and the massive Chateau Lake Louise Hotel.

Crooked Bush

Stop snickering. This gnarly grove of oddly mutated aspens near Hafford, Saskatchewan, reportedly makes visitors feel ill, and some people report feeling strange vibrations from the earth. Among the more colourful (and pungent) explanations for the trees is that alien visitors have peed on them.

Scarborough Bluffs

Running for 14 kilometres along the shore of Lake Ontario, the bluffs are massive cliffs of sedimentary deposits that have never fully fused into rock. They are renowned as a geological wonder for providing an unusually complete record of local glaciation.

Flowerpot Monoliths

Québec's Mingan Archipelago and Ontario's Tobermory region are home to these rock formation also known as "sea stacks."

Eroded over millions of years, the "flowerpots" are the wide, mushroom-like caps of the slender rock pillars below.

Rocher Percé

For the Anglos in the crowd, it's "Percé Rock," the monolithic slab of stone just off the shore of the town of Percé in Québec. The arches worn through the rock by seawater are probably responsible for its name, *percé* being French for "pierced" or "perforated."

Zecs

In many ways, zecs are humanmade natural wonders—the word describes privately funded nature reserves in *la belle province*.

Old Sow Whirlpool

The largest tidal whirlpool in the Western Hemisphere, Old Sow in Passamaquoddy Bay, New Brunswick, is surrounded by numerous smaller whirlpools, nicknamed "piglets."

Reversing Falls

No illusion in Saint John, New Brunswick; the water really does flow backward, but they are not so much falls as they are swiftly moving rapids, caused by the Bay of Fundy's high tide cresting 4 metres higher than the St. John River, which flows into it, thus violently pushing the river water back upstream.

Magnetic Hill

Famous all across the land, this optical illusion in Moncton, New Brunswick, is no less awesome for knowing it is an illusion. Because of the rolling terrain and partially obscured horizon, vehicles in neutral gear appear to roll *uphill!*

Peggy's Cove

Famous for having the most photographed lighthouse in Canada (possibly the world), Peggy's Cove in Nova Scotia is also remarkable for its barren lunar landscape scraped clean by the glaciers, which also deposited huge and seemingly out-of-place boulders as they retreated.

Bay of Fundy

Besides being a treasure trove for fishing and oceanography, this famous body of water between New Brunswick and Nova Scotia is also well known for having the highest tides in the world, cresting at more than 15 metres and in some cases exceeding 16 metres.

Grand Banks

This series of massive underwater plateaus in Newfoundland is partly responsible for Canada's once-thriving fishing industry and so, much of our history. They're also a boon to birders and whale watchers.

Singing Sand, PEI

Really, it should be called "squeaking sand" for the distinctive
gritty squeak the sand makes when you step heavily on it or dig
in your foot. It may have something to do with the grains of quartz
sand, which are rounder than normal sand.

NATURE AWESOME SUPERSIZE

It's not just that Canada has awesome natural scenery and attractions—it's that so many of them are so big. In fact, some of Canada's most famous "regions" are larger than many European countries and contain within them so much awesomeness that the only way to fit a fraction of them into this book is to encapsulate.

Yukon Wildlife Preserve

Get ready for wildlife! Moose, bison, elk, caribou, mountain goats, deer, Dall's sheep, muskox and lynx all find happy homes in spacious enclosures.

Rankin Inlet

This remote community in Nunavut is awesome not only for its proximity to Iqalugaarjuup Nunanga Territorial Park but also for the Kangirqliniq Center for Arts and Learning, which is notable as a production centre for Inuit ceramic fine arts.

Great Slave Lake

At 614 metres, this lake in the Northwest Territories is Canada's deepest, adding further to its reputation as a still mysterious giant of the north. Macedonia would fit comfortably inside it.

Great Bear Lake

The Northwest Territories also has the largest lake contained entirely within Canada—you could plonk Belgium in it and still have a bit of room left for overflow.

Tundra

This type of terrain covers much of northern Canada and is notable for its rocky outcrops, lack of trees and inevitable permafrost. While it is decidedly inhospitable, many see it as emblematic of a certain aspect of the Canadian character—tough and able to persevere in harsh conditions.

Whistler

This notable example in BC of the awesome result of humanity meeting nature offers some of the finest skiing in the world, pleasant accommodations and an Olympic heritage, having hosted the 2010 Winter Games.

Okanagan Valley

As so often happens, it's difficult to compress the awesomeness of this BC valley into a little blurb, but here goes: beautiful scenery, fruit orchards, vineyards, charming resorts and the inevitable tug of history.

Fraser River

Flowing for 1375 kilometres, the Fraser River passes through some of BC's most beautiful scenery and challenging terrain.

Purcell Mountains

Sure, everyone's heard of the Rockies and the Laurentians, but the Purcells? They're a subrange of the Columbia Mountains in BC, awesome for their rocky granite formations improbably called "the Bugaboos." Given the Bugaboos' silly name, seeing them can be a bit of a shock. They're not silly at all; they're massive, towering chunks of granite that jut up majestically out of the ground. Amazingly, but arguably not awesomely, at some point in our nation's past, someone thought it was a good idea to name the surrounding area Bugaboo Provincial Park. Seriously?

Stanley Park

By far my favourite thing about this "tamed wilderness" park in Vancouver (a lot of big trees but also bike trails) is that you can literally stumble upon massive tree stumps carved into beautiful totem figures.

Great Bear Rainforest

Cited by many as one of the largest, intact, temperate rainforests in the world, it is often called "Canada's Amazon." Besides a rich array of flora and fauna, this park in BC is also home to the rare white Kermode Spirit Bear, from whence comes the rainforest's name. Covering 70,000 square kilometres, Great Bear Rainforest is about the size of Ireland but almost certainly has fewer Irish.

Rocky Mountains

If you don't already think the Rocky Mountains in BC and Alberta are awesome, then a few lines of text aren't going to convince you.

The Prairies

There is much that is awesome about the Prairies, but for first-time visitors, the most surprising thing is sure to be the landscape, the huge dome of the sky, the enormous sense of flatness and indefinable nature of sunlight uninterrupted by buildings or trees. The *feel* of the Prairies is different from anywhere else in Canada.

Badlands

Dry, dusty, rocky and closely resembling the background of a Roadrunner and Coyote cartoon, badlands are strange, alien places found in Alberta and Saskatchewan. They excel at having dinosaur fossils.

Banff National Park

Founded in 1885, this park in Alberta was Canada's first national park. Encompassing more than 6600 square kilometres (larger than the Palestinian Territories) of spectacular mountains and wildlife, the scenery is truly breathtaking. But if you're a fan of glaciers, you'd better visit soon, since they're visibly melting.

Red River

As well as lending its name to a popular brand of cracked wheat hot cereal, the Red River in Manitoba is inexorably and tragically linked with the shaping of Canada's history through the events of the Red River Resistance of 1869.

Algonquin Park

A few of the attractions: great canoeing, unspoiled wilderness and excellent camping all packed into a measly 7630 square kilometres in Ontario. (The park is as big as Puerto Rico, since now, apparently, I've started something.)

Thousand Islands

Teeming with cottagers and tourists but none the worse for it, the St. Lawrence River's Thousand Islands in Ontario comprise 1865 islands, but clearly that would be bit of a mouthful and probably a drain on the local economy.

Thirty Thousand Islands

If you've ever wondered why the Group of Seven painted the way they did, just visit Georgian Bay, see a few of the Thirty Thousand Islands and you will get the idea. Like their fractional relations, the Thousand Islands, the Thirty Thousand Islands in Ontario are also infested with humanity, but there's still more than enough stirring natural beauty to go round.

Manitoulin Island

The multiple layers of awesomeness in this Ontario island start with a population that's 25 percent First Nations and continue with the awesome scenery and 110 inland lakes (that's right—lakes on an island, which is itself in a lake) but don't end with this startling geo-fact: Manitoulin is the world's largest freshwater island, which is to say it's the world's largest island situated in a lake.

The Great Lakes

I know there are five of them, but I'm counting the Great Lakes in Ontario as one awesome thing. Anyway, I think we all know the routine: 20 percent of the world's freshwater spread out over 244,000 square kilometres, ecosystems, wildlife, trade routes, stories, legends—they're the *Great Lakes* for cryin' out loud.

Haliburton Highlands

With forests, lakes and other natural sites, the Haliburton Highlands in Ontario are awesome all year round. You can hike, fish and go on boating or tree canopy tours in the summer, and ski, snowboard and go dogsledding in the winter.

The Muskokas

This area in Ontario has lovely woods, countryside, wetlands, lakes, fishing, boating, sightseeing and nice places to stay. No more. No less.

Canadian Shield

Covering 4.8 million square kilometres, this massive Precambrian rock formation is probably one of the country's best known geological features, having influenced most of Canadian history and sporting a name that inspires feelings of patriotism.

Gaspé Peninsula

This region of eastern Québec is approximately the size of Belgium. Among its many awesome features are the Chic Choc Mountains, rustic fishing villages and whale watching, as well as numerous nature reserves and parks.

Nunavik

Described by some as "Canada's last frontier" (whatever that's supposed to mean), Nunavik in northern Québec is certainly remote. About the size of Spain, it is sparsely populated with various Inuit settlements and herds of caribou and muskox.

Laurentian Mountains

They might have been talking about the Laurentians in Québec when they coined the phrase "as old as the mountains." Besides lending their name to a popular brand of pencil crayons, at 500 million years old (probably more), the Laurentians are recognized as one of the oldest mountain systems in the world.

James Bay

Roughly equal in size to Germany, James Bay in Québec is a hydroelectric powerhouse with 215 dams that help to pump out almost 16,000 megawatts of energy.

Avalon Peninsula

A delight for whale- and birdwatchers in Newfoundland, but also for historians, with Castle Hill National Historic Site and its

17th-century French fortifications, as well as an interpretive centre for ongoing archaeological digs. Cape St. Mary's Ecological Reserve is a pleasant stop, too.

Bonavista Peninsula

Get your all-encompassing taste of Atlantic Canada here. There are eccentric town names in Newfoundland and Labrador, such as Birchy Cove and Trouty, as well as a national historic site dedicated to the fishing industry, the likely spot where explorer John Cabot stepped ashore and, not surprisingly, traditional minstrelsy and diverse entertainments.

Two Million Lakes

According to Government of Canada websites (which are *always* reliable and *always* provide sources—as if), Canada has two million lakes. Good luck trying to find the survey, report or wild guesstimate that originally said this. It seems to have become part of the accepted lore about our country, but I, for one, remain skeptical, largely because this "fact" just seems to float around out there with no indication as to who first put it forth. It would be awesome if it *were* true—and I hope it is.

OUT OF THE ORDINARY

Canada can be glad that it was not dubbed with some of the other names suggested at the time of Confederation. While a few of the names were submitted in jest (or what passed for jesting in 1867), I think you will agree that we can all be glad we do not live in Albertsland, Albionara, Borealia, Britannia, Cabotia, Mesopelagia, Norland, Superior, Transatlantia, Tupona (an acronym for The United Provinces of North America), Victorialand and, saving the worst for last, my personal favourite, Efisga (an acronym for England, France, Ireland, Scotland, Germany and Aborigines).

Fortunately, all joking aside, calm heads prevailed, and it was decided to simply call the new nation what everyone had been calling it since the 1500s anyway—Canada. Although the country itself escaped with its dignity intact, the following generations of might-have-been Efisgians in no way demonstrated similar restraint when naming their towns and cities. Some of these place names will be known to you already and others will not. Some are obviously funny, and others, frankly, simply strike me as odd. You may or may not agree. Please direct all correspondence to the publisher.

Yukon

Champagne

Destruction Bay

Flat Top

Hungry Lake

Mount Cockfield

Nogold Creek

Snafu Creek

Snag

Northwest Territories

Reliance

The Ramparts

Thumb Island

Nunavut

Air Force Island

Chesterfield Inlet

Eureka

Repulse Island

Resolute

British Columbia

Bugaboo Provincial Park

Chilliwack

Kamloops

Alberta

Drumheller

Head-Smashed-In Buffalo Jump

Medicine Hat

Saskatchewan

Biggar

Bimbo (a school district)

Climax

Fertile

Forget

Love

Superb

Tisdale (This town's name isn't weird, but the city's motto, "Land of Rape and Honey," is guaranteed to raise eyebrows. The motto refers to rapeseed.)

Manitoba

Ebb and Flow

Flin Flon

Nonsuch

Mechanic Settlement

Passamaquoddy Bay

Poodiac

Ontario

Biggles	Nipissing
Bummer's Roost	Scugog
Cobalt	Swastika
East Garafraxa	Punkeydoodles Corners
Moose Factory	Upper Big Chute
Moosonee	Warburg

Québec

Chicoutimi

Saint-Louis-du-Ha! Ha!

Tadoussac

New Brunswick

Beersville	Cocagne
Bouctouche	Quispamsis
Burnt Church	Roachville

Prince Edward Island

Crapaud

Pisquid

Nova Scotia

Antigonish	Mushaboom
Ecum Secum	Shag Harbour
Garden of Eden	Ulva
Lower Economy	Yankeetown

Newfoundland and Labrador

Bumblebee Bight

Come By Chance

Gargamelle

Goobies

Happy Adventure

Happy Valley Goosebay

Heart's Content

Leading Tickles

Little Seldom

Nameless Cove

Pippy Park

Tilting

Too Good Arm

Quidi Vidi Village

Quirpon

CAPITAL ASSETS

Since middle school, we've learned about the riches of Canada's natural resources. In some cases they are non-renewable, which means that once we've dug them out the ground and used them up, they won't be coming back (not within our lifetimes or our children's or our children's children's or…you get the idea). Some of our natural resources are renewable, and occasionally the efforts at renewal become an industry in and of themselves. Here, with little commentary, since we're all familiar with their awesomeness, are some of our country's economic staples.

Oil Patch

Calling Canada's largely prairie-based petroleum industry the "Oil Patch" makes it sound like folksy little Petro Fairies are bouncing around in a magical land of…oil, but between the tar sands and conventional production, Canada pumps out almost three million barrels *a day* (much of which comes from "The Patch").

Potash

Thanks mainly to Saskatchewan, Canada is the world's largest single exporter of potash (used in fertilizer), accounting for 43 percent of the world's trade. Put that in your pot and grow it!

Mines

Gold, silver, frankincense and myrrh—you name it, we mine it. Seriously, though, nix the frankincense and myrrh, add nickel, iron, uranium and cobalt, and you get a fair picture of Canada's awesome mining clout.

Hydro

No, we're not talking about BC hydroponic pot (though some would argue that West Coast hoolie is one of Canada's most economically important exports). Rather, we're talking about hydro-electric energy, something we produce in great abundance.

Forestry

We have a lot of trees. We chop them down and make stuff out of them.

Tree Planting

The notion of replanting our forests is all very well, but the *experience* of tree planting has become a rite of passage for many young Canadians who sign up for a summer of back-breaking work and good money, all in remote locations with a group of their peers from whom they cannot escape. Apparently, tree planting will either break your spirit or make you realize you can overcome pretty much anything life may throw at you.

Saskatchewan Forestry

I know we've already tipped our tuques to forestry and tree planting in general, but from the "Who'd a Thunk It?" file comes this surprising (to me) factoid: in Saskatchewan, a Prairie province, nearly *one quarter* of the land is covered by commercial forests. That's an area the size of Germany, in case you were missing the geographic belittling of European nations.

FEATHERS, FUR AND FLIPPERS

Canada is justly famous for its fascinating birds and animals, some of which seem to have that extra something that makes them not merely fascinating but awesome. It may be the pleasantly nationalistic associations they possess or they may conjure stirring notions of nature—or they may simply poop a lot.

Pelicans

Most people imagine pelicans as the denizens of sun-soaked southern piers. Saskatchewan is the last place you'd expect to see these large, pouch-billed birds, but they've been sighted in the province since 1879.

Puffins

A large colony of these famously ground-dwelling birds is at Witless Bay, Newfoundland and Labrador (being the official bird of same). The triangular eye markings of puffins appear to give them "sympathetic" expressions that tug at the heartstrings of tender-hearted observers. They are awesomely cute.

Chicken Chariot Races

If you're not suitably impressed with Canada's impressive fowl species in their natural state, you can always take a trip to Saskatchewan to watch the locals in Wynard blow off some steam at the Chicken Chariot Races. As you might expect, this awesomely eccentric sport involves tying miniature chariots to chickens and seeing which one can run the fastest.

Ducks

Everybody loves ducks. They're one of the first birds that toddlers learn to recognize, and they are as delightful in Canada as anywhere. Saskatchewan also plays nursery to approximately one-quarter of the ducks in North America.

Thompson Turkeys

Ravens in Thompson, Manitoba, are large, smart birds famous for plucking plastic bags out of unsecured garbage cans, dropping them on the street until they break open and sorting through the wreckage for the good bits. The crafty avians have been awesomely nicknamed "Thompson turkeys."

Bears

Polar, grizzly, brown or black, Canadians love their bears, perhaps because bears exhibit behaviour that many Canadians would like to emulate: end the summer being fat and well fed on a diet of honey, berries and salmon and then hibernate for the winter and wake up a few months later, relatively thin and ready for love.

Beavers

It's arguable that if Canada didn't have beavers, the country as we know it would not exist today. Our early history is founded on the nearly extinct killing of beavers to make hats out of their skins. The world's second largest rodent (after the capybara) is known as "nature's engineer" for its prodigious diligence in building dams and lodges, which some fondly imagine reflects our national character as ingenious, hardworking exploiters of natural resources. These are the reasons that this toothy, flat-tailed creature appears on our nickels and is our national symbol.

Tree-climbing Mountain Beavers

Though they rarely do, some beavers can climb trees. Since their name is a strikingly complete and accurate description of what makes these animals awesome, any further comment on my part would be redundant.

Buffalo

Once 60 million strong, the North America bison was hunted almost to extinction with the arrival of white settlers. But a First Nations animal breeder called Walking Coyote had maintained a small breeding herd that grew and was eventually purchased by Canada, in a surprising instance of a government taking action before it was too late.

Chipmunks

Cute, chirpy and laugh-out-loud funny when stuffing their cheeks with food, chipmunks are an awesome sight for anyone new to Canada's northlands, as well as those long accustomed to their inquisitive and slightly indignant personalities.

Dinosaurs

No, not living dinosaurs, rather, their massive, fossilized bones found in awesome profusion and diversity in Alberta and Saskatchewan.

Newfoundland Dogs

Big, black, fat and friendly, these grinning, drooly dogs are magnificent furry beasts, capable of swimming for hours and possessing awesome canine strength. One such dog, called Bonzo Bear, pulled a 2000-kilogram weight to make it into the *Guinness Book of World Records*. Another, called Tang, was reputedly given a life-saving medal after swimming ashore with the rescue line of a capsized ship.

Dolphins

Dolphins are indisputably cool, but the surprising fact (to me) that they live in Canadian waters is truly awesome. The bottle-nosed variety can be seen in the waters of both New Brunswick and Nova Scotia.

Foxes

The bane of farmers everywhere, foxes are a delight to otherwise city-bound cottagers, with their quiet, unassuming personalities and fine features (the foxes, not the cottagers). Sometimes you can be sitting out on the porch reading in the setting sun, and you look up to see a fox silently sitting in the shadows just watching (and probably waiting to see if you're going to put any food out).

Lynxes

Truly cool cats, lynxes are most easily recognized by the spire-like tufts that look like radio antennae on the tops of their ears. A lynx appears on the 1967 centennial quarter.

Moose

Not unique to Canada, but somehow distinctly Canadian, moose often appear on highways as driving hazards, but not at all on our quarters, which are graced by caribou. An awesome moose fact: their giant antlers grow back every year, giving them the fastest growing tissue system in the world.

Possums

Often thought of as animals of the Deep South, possums have been playing dead and showing Ontarians the whites of their eyes for the last few decades.

Raccoons

Familiar to suburbanites and cottagers as brash, dexterous pests that are simultaneously annoying and cute, raccoons are nonetheless awesome creatures, being highly adaptable, surprisingly agile and having 10,000 times as many nerve endings in their paws as do human hands.

River Otters

During winter, these furry, fast-moving animals can be spotted sliding across patches of snow and ice, most likely because it takes less energy than walking, in such a manner that humans would call "playful."

Salamanders

Don't think salamanders are awesome? Then pay a visit to Saltcoats, Saskatchewan—the self-proclaimed Salamander Capital of Canada. Their sheer numbers will change your mind.

Shark Watching

Everyone talks about watching whales, but for the carnivorously minded, Lunenburg, Nova Scotia's Ocean Adventures gives you the awesomely unexpected chance to go shark watching—you're protected by a cage that is lowered into the ocean waters (oh, you also have to be a licensed scuba diver).

Snakes

I'm not talking about the run-of-the-mill variety of venomous and non-venomous snakes that reside in Canada, but rather, the giant underground pits full of thousands upon thousands of red-sided garter snakes near Narcisse, Manitoba. Nothing says awesome like subterranean snake pits.

Squirrels

Boy, does Canada have squirrels. Squirrels are awesome for being much easier to tame than chipmunks. As someone who has done both, you can take my word for it.

White Squirrels

Exeter, Ontario, boasts not merely pink-eyed albino squirrels, but rather, black-eyed white squirrels. And the Toronto neighbourhood near Queen St. West and Ossington is infamous for unconfirmed sightings of white squirrels on the grounds of the Canadian Association for Mental Health.

Whales

You can watch the whales on either the East or the West Coast, and the chance to see some of nature's biggest creatures is never anything less than awesome.

Wild Horses of Sable Island

Whether they swam ashore after shipwrecks or were deliberately left on Sable Island during the Acadian Expulsion, the horses are one of Canada's wildest, most majestic and largely unseen attractions—but it's nice to know they're there.

Wolves

Maybe it's because there are still places in Canada where you can howl at the moon and hear wolves howl back (seriously), but for many Canadians, wolves represent a connection to the wild, primal place that Canada once was and still is.

STRENGTH IN DIVERSITY

How different would Canada be if one or more of the following groups was absent from our history and culture? Many of the opinions expressed herein are for humorous effect only, while others are deadly serious. I leave it to you, gentle reader, to decide which are which.

First Nations

Besides being the first Canadians, the First Nations continue to influence this country with the adoption of Aboriginal societal models such as using conflict and sentencing circles. And let's not forget the five Ojibwa functions of humanity: leading, defending, providing, healing and teaching.

Inuit

In many ways the Inuit defined Canada in the eyes of outsiders—we're all "Eskimos" who live in igloos. In less trivial ways, their knowledge and traditions continue to shape Canada as a nation and Canadians as a people.

Haida

The Haida gave us the style of woodcarving that, to many people, *is* Canadian First Nations art. Beyond that, their influence and knowledge had, and continues to have, a huge impact on the settling and development of coastal BC.

Ukrainians

Just think, without the 170,000 Ukrainians who came to Canada between 1891 and 1914, we probably wouldn't love kubasa and Ukrainian Easter eggs (*pysanky*) the way we do. Not only that, but we also wouldn't have the giant Easter egg in Vegreville, Alberta.

French

Besides bringing their Gallic *joi de vivre*, the French were leaders at killing anything with fur and sending the pelts to Europe to get made into hats. Without the French, we wouldn't have poutine, *sacres* and French labels on food.

Scottish

When the Scots arrived, they brought with them their hardiness, frugality, love of golf and, as Stephen Leacock says, "their comprehensive views on damnation." Without the Scots, it is doubtful that each Canadian province would have its own tartan.

THE CULTURAL MELTING POT

The English brought with them the oppressive colonial outlook, general tight-assery, prudish mores, WASP tendencies and slavish devotion to a distant monarch, all of which seep back into Canadian society more and more every day.

Irish

The Irish brought with them a bloody-minded attitude necessary to survive in a country ruled by two pompous, prosperous and imperialistic nations. While the English and French fought over supremacy, the Irish went to work catching fish to feed the armies. Without the Irish, Atlantic Canada would look very different, and Newfoundland English wouldn't sound the way it does.

Acadians

Arguably Canada's "French Irish," the Acadians were expelled from Canada under the yolk of British imperialism, but thanks to their pervasive influence, we tend to think of traditional "French Canadian" culture as rustic, charming and homey, rather than high-falutin' ermine-trimmed, gilded grandiosity.

Chinese

It is well known that the Canadian Pacific Railway was built in large part by Chinese labourers, but more significantly, Chinese immigrants were Canada's first significant influx from Asia and in many ways laid the foundation for the cultural patchwork that Canadian cities would soon become.

INVITED INTERLOPERS (MOSTLY)

With a national character shaped by many disparate cultures, Canada is perhaps more than typically open to foreign powers and potentates setting up shop in our home. It's not that we're giving away the store so much as being open to lending out space—after all, space is what we have the most of.

Chinese Air Force School

Sponsored by the Chinese National League, the Keng Wah Aviation School opened its doors in Saskatoon in 1919. It trained more than 200 pilots on behalf of Sino revolutionary Sun Yat-sen.

Ottawa Tulip Festival

Ever wonder why we have a tulip festival? In 1940, Holland's Princess Julia fled the Nazis and came to Canada. When it was time for the birth of her third daughter, a maternity ward at Ottawa Civic Hospital was temporarily declared Dutch soil, and the Dutch flag was briefly raised over Parliament—all so the new princess could be a Dutch citizen. At the end of the war, a grateful, and now reinstated, Royal Family sent 100,000 tulip bulbs to Canada.

Little Norway

First opening in 1940 on the shores of Lake Ontario near Toronto's Island Airport and later moving to Muskoka, Little Norway was a training facility for pilots of the Royal Norwegian Air force after Norway's 1940 defeat by Germany. About 2500 Norwegian pilots trained at the two locations.

Camp X

In 1941, infamous Canadian spymaster William Stephenson set up this secret facility near Whitby, Ontario. British commandos secretly taught sabotage and spycraft to U.S. agents, since the United States was still officially neutral and not yet fighting in World War II.

Commonwealth Air Training Plan

During World War II, British, Australian, Kiwi and Canadian fighter pilots trained at more than 100 schools across Canada. The program employed nearly 11,000 aircraft and more than 100,000 ground personnel.

Little Reich on the Prairie

In February 1942, Nazis took over the city of Winnipeg, staged a book burning, arrested the mayor and renamed their new prize "Himmlerstadt." Fortunately, it was all a well-publicized drive to sell Victory Bonds, and at 5:30 PM, the "Nazis" took off their uniforms and once more became Canadians.

Weather Station Kurt

In October 1943, a German crew landed in Labrador's far north and installed an antennae, sensor equipment and batteries to broadcast meteorological information back to Germany. The only armed Nazi military operation on North American soil was then forgotten about until the early 1980s, when a German archivist discovered

Kurt's records and notified some Canadians, who promptly went out and found it. Kurt stands today in the Canadian War Museum in Ottawa.

St. Pierre et Miquelon

Twenty-five kilometres from the southern shores of Newfoundland lie these two tiny French islands. Not only do their residents speak French, but France owns the islands, and if you go there, you're technically in France. Yes, they *do* have a guillotine, in case you were wondering.

SEEING IS BELIEVING

Jesus' Face Appears at Tim Hortons

Yup, the face of Jesus briefly appeared on the outside brick wall of a Tim Hortons in Cape Breton in 1998. The image quickly vanished, but not before Mary Magdalene showed up on a Timbit and the archangel Gabriel appeared on the flipside of a macadamia nut cookie. No, not really, but seriously, somebody did say that the face of Jesus had appeared on the wall at Timmy Ho's.

Virgin Mary Appears in a Greenhouse Window

On September 8, 2002, many residents of the little prairie town of Ile a la Crosse, Saskatchewan, were celebrating the Feast of the Birth of the Blessed Virgin Mary. That day and for the next several days, images of the Virgin Mary and other sacred symbols appeared in the condensation between two panes of glass in a local greenhouse. The images came and went, sometimes morphing into the sacred heart, a chalice or an angel. Numerous witness reported having seen the images, and all agreed there was a flash of light in the sky when the visions ceased.

Serpent Mound

At the tip of Rice Lake in Ontario is the Serpent Mound. Whether it was ever really shaped like a serpent is debatable, but what's not in doubt is that it is a burial mound for several different generations of First Nations ancestors, the Hopewell Group, who flourished from about 200 BCE to 500 CE. Serpent Mounds Park (there are also several smaller mounds or "eggs" surrounding the main formation) is now a National Historic Site.

Pilot Mound

The town of Pilot Mound, Manitoba, is named after a large mound that was present at the town's first site, before the residents decided to move the town closer to the newly laid CPR tracks. A 1908 archaeological dig found that, like Ontario's Serpent Mound, Manitoba's was also a burial site for long deceased First Nations progenitors.

Petroglyphs Provincial Park

In the early 1950s, a prospector discovered a massive shelf of white marble pushing up through the undergrowth near Peterborough, Ontario. On it were more than 900 symbols and fantastical figures, all carved or scratched into the surface by hands long gone. The otherworldly figures are likely representations of visions seen during spirit quests. An interpretive centre has been constructed over the white marble shelf to protect the petroglyphs, and you can visit the site to share in the visions of spiritual travellers from long ago.

St. Victor Petroglyphs

About 300 symbols and figures are carved on a huge crag of sandstone near St. Victor, Saskatchewan. Estimated to be between 300 and 1000 years old, the petroglyphs are fast disappearing as a result of the ceaseless hand of nature. A movement was afoot to somehow preserve them, but local First Nations elders visited the site and requested that nature be allowed to take its course and slowly wear the symbols away. The truly awesome thing about this story is that the town is complying with the elders' wishes!

Tramping Lake Petroglyphs

The other petroglyphs described herein are cut or scratched into the stone, but the survival of the ones at Tramping Lake, Manitoba, is all the more awesome because the people who painted them between 1500 to 3000 years ago did so by dipping their fingers in red ochre and daubing it onto the rock face, allowing us to literally touch the past.

Medicine Wheels

There are only about 175 of these large, circular arrangements of rocks and boulders left in North America. Sacred to all the Plains tribes, medicine wheels were ceremonial places of group prayer, meditation and communion with the spirits. Most have a cairn or boulder at the centre with arrangements of smaller stones radiating out from the centre. The most prominent medicine wheels still visible today are all on the Prairies.

☛ Moose Mountain: This medicine wheel in Manitoba is about 800 years old but possibly has older formations buried under the visible one.

☛ Tie Creek: This medicine wheel, also in Manitoba, is so big that its diameter is measured in *kilometres*; its age is unknown.

☛ Big Muddy Badlands: Estimated to be 5000 years old, this kidney-shaped medicine wheel in Saskatchewan may have gotten its shape from being partially covered.

☛ Wanuskewin Heritage Park: Also in Saskatchewan, this 6000-year-old site of pre–First Nations activity has a medicine wheel 1500 years old and 21 metres across.

CLASSICALLY CANADIAN

It comes as no surprise that we Canucks are a literary bunch. After all, before the advent of radio, TV and subsequent electronic entertainments, much of Canada's history was defined by long winter nights with nothing better to do than read, write and have sex…hmm, maybe, in that case, it is surprising that we're such a lettered bunch. Anyway, what follows is an attempt to mix the obvious with the unexpected and is by no means intended to be comprehensive.

Strange Manuscript Found in a Copper Cylinder

Canada's first science-fiction novel was published in 1888. Written by James De Mille, founder of Dalhousie University's department of English, it tells the story of a sailor who washes ashore to discover a society that regards death as the greatest boon that one person can bestow upon another.

Anne of Green Gables

Starting in 1908, author Lucy Maud Montgomery introduced the world to Anne Shirley of PEI, she of the red hair, green window trimmings and a popularity that shows no sign of abating.

"In Flanders Fields"

Written by Lieutenant Colonel John McRae, this war poem became an "instant classic" upon its composition in 1915. Recognized in English-speaking countries the world over, it is arguably the principal reason we wear poppies in the days surrounding Remembrance Day. While "Lest We Forget" is the more poetic expression of the sentiment, I prefer (and aver that) "We Shall Never Forget."

Alligator Pie and Garbage Delight

Written by Toronto Poet Laureate Dennis Lee, these two works of short, simple and funny rhymes for kids lifted children's verse out of the past (dairy maids, tuffets, curds and whey) and placed them firmly in the everyday world of the 1970s (string, popsicles, hockey and bologna), much to the delight of generations since.

WRITERS

Skaay (b. 1827–?)

Known in English as John Sky, Skaay was a Haida poet and story-teller who told a transcribed version of the Raven myth that is among the longest and most complete in the West Coast tradition. His other central work is a 5500-line epic poem called the "Qquuna Cycle."

Ghandl (b. 1851–?)

Known in English as Walter McGregor and called by some the "Homer" of Haida oral storytelling, Ghandl left behind an impressive body of work transcribed by cultural archivist John Swanton and later translated by Robert Bringhurst. Ghandl's voice is held in high esteem as a shining example of the pre-European Haida tradition. Bringhurst has courted controversy by suggesting that some Haida myths and stories are not anonymous oral myths but creative works of specific individuals such as Ghandl and Skaay.

E. Pauline Johnson (1861–1913)

Also known as Tekahionwake ("double-life"), Johnson was the daughter of a Mohawk chief and an English immigrant. While her best-known work today is probably the poem "The Song My Paddle Sings" (circa 1892), during her lifetime, she was also highly regarded as a recitationist, or what we might today call "a spoken-word artist."

Robert Service (1874–1958)

Called "the Canadian Kipling," Service is remembered today for poems such as "The Shooting of Dan McGrew" (1907) and that perennial elementary school public-speaking favourite, "The Cremation of Sam McGee" (1907).

Robertson Davies (1913–95)

This prolific and towering literary figure puts to shame those of us who toil away grinding out books of trivia. Aside from a career that encompassed journalism, editing, playwriting, directing theatre, literary criticism and teaching, he is probably most widely remembered for his novel trilogies: *The Salterton Trilogy* (1951–58), *The Deptford Trilogy* (1970–75) and *The Cornish Trilogy* (1981–88).

Pierre Berton (1920–2004)

The writer who made the world realize that Canadian history could be exciting, Berton published countless volumes of lively, meticulously researched "popular history." While many of his works are famous in Canada, his two-volume history of the War of 1812—*The Invasion of Canada* (1980) and *Flames Across the Border* (1981)—in particular shows a non-fiction writer at the height of his powers.

Farley Mowat (b. 1921)

Often exploring themes of nature conservation, Mowat's work is always humorous, conversational and fast-paced. *Never Cry Wolf* (1963) is probably the work he is best known for, but his children's books, *The Dog Who Wouldn't Be* (1957), *Owls in the Family* (1961) and *The Boat Who Wouldn't Float* (1969), are also regarded as classics.

Margaret Laurence (1926–87)

Probably best known for her novels *The Stone Angel* (1964) and *The Diviners* (1974), Laurence's work looks at the changing choices (and voices) of women in Canada in the mid-20th century.

Mordecai Richler (1931–2001)

An excellent example of the writer as likable curmudgeon, Richler was a novelist and essayist who could always be relied upon to have a strong opinion. A few of many notable works are *The Apprenticeship of Duddy Kravitz* (1969), *Solomon Gursky Was Here* (1989) and *Barney's Version* (1997).

Alice Munro (b. 1931)

This three-time winner of the Governor General's Award is known for her often thematically linked short stories. Munro's work often features small epiphanies that lend significance to external events; in other words, much of the action is internal.

Margaret Atwood (b. 1939)

Arguably Canada's best-known writer, Atwood is a novelist, essayist and poet, notable for an incredibly diverse body of work that trades in themes of feminism, Canadian identity, sexual identity and just being human.

Michael Ondaatje (b. 1943)

Sri Lankan–born Ondaatje won the Booker Prize for his 1992 novel, *The English Patient*, but is also known for such earlier works as *Coming Through the Slaughter* (1976) and *In the Skin of a Lion* (1987), to which *The English Patient* is a partial sequel.

Robert Munsch (b. 1945)

This bestselling children's author and storyteller got his start working with preschool children and telling them tall tales that took place in the everyday world. Thirty million books sold later, he is now one of Canada's most successful cultural exports. Notable works include *The Paper Bag Princess* (1980) and *Love You Forever* (1986).

Tomson Highway (b. 1951)

Canada's foremost Cree playwright is the author of *The Rez Sisters* (1986) and *Drylips Oughta Move to Kapuskasing* (1989), as well as the novel *Kiss of the Fur Queen* (1998). He has won numerous awards and honours for his work.

Douglas Coupland (b. 1961)

Besides popularizing the term "Generation X" (and giving us a 1991 novel of the same name), Coupland has had a prolific career as a novelist and graphic artist.

Malcolm Gladwell (b. 1963)

The bestselling non-fiction author of such works as *The Tipping Point: How Little Things Make a Big Difference* (2000), *Blink: The Power of Thinking Without Thinking* (2005) and *Outliers: The Story of Success* (2008) elucidates often unexpected ideas in over-looked conceptual spaces.

BEEN THERE, DONE THAT

Canadians pop up in some of the strangest, least expected and, occasionally, most dangerous corners of the earth. Making our influence felt doesn't necessarily mean going abroad, but it may entail joining august bodies or planting the maple leaf where it can't fail to be noticed.

The Canadian Caper

During the Iran Hostage Crisis of 1979–80, Canadian ambassador to Iran, Ken Taylor, along with the CIA, hatched a plot to smuggle out six U.S. diplomats under the guise of a film crew making a dreadful science-fiction movie. The 2012 Hollywood movie *Argo*, which recounted these events, predictably minimized the initiative and personal risk undertaken by Ken Taylor, instead representing the whole thing as the outcome of "Uhmurrican Injuhnooity."

University of the Arctic

Founded in 2001, the University of the Arctic is co-operative network of 143 universities from countries with territories in the polar region. It's motto is, "In the North, by the North, for the North." Canada is a member, along with Denmark, Finland, Iceland, Norway, Russia, Sweden and the U.S. (Alaska).

Maple Leaf Pub

This pub in London, England, is decorated in a Canadian theme, with hockey jerseys, a Mountie uniform, paddles, a stuffed moose head and other artifacts that English people think represent Canada. They also serve a wide selection of Canadian beers. While ex-pats abroad can stop in for a taste of home, the clientele is much like that of any other pub in central London.

COMPANIES AND ENTERPRISES

Canadians aren't just good at making maple syrup, making music and making people laugh; we're also very good at making money, sometimes through maple syrup, music and laughter. Canada itself is founded on ingenuity, ambition and a healthy dash of rapacious corporate greed. Fish and fur were the early engines of the Canadian economy, but the years since have been amply populated by entrepreneurs out to make a buck.

Hudson's Bay Company

Founded in 1670, the HBC is the oldest operating commercial entity in North America and one of the oldest in the world. Although it was more of an empire than a retailer, the HBC is now a ubiquitous Canadian department store, the Bay. Besides owning most of Canada throughout its early history, the HBC shaped Canada's history as the dominant fur traders of their day.

Card Money

In the late 17th and early 18th centuries, there was a serious lack of gold in New France. An ingenious bureaucrat cut up some playing cards, initialled them and announced that they would henceforth be treated as legal tender, redeemable for gold when the next shipment arrived from France. Go fish!

Canpotex

Since 1972, this company has been Canada's leading exporter of potash. Whether you believe it is a "cartel" or not, the brilliance of a model that gives one company a virtual monopoly on overseas exports is undeniably awesome, regardless of whether it is "fair" or not.

Canadian Tire Money

When you buy something at Canadian Tire, you get a percentage of the value of your purchase back in redeemable paper bills that feel frustratingly like real money to hopeful fingers in pockets. Though really nothing more than a customer loyalty program, it is a source of bafflement to most new arrivals to Canada.

BlackBerry

Starting corporate life as RIM (Research In Motion, founded in 1995), BlackBerry undeniably changed the world with its awesome line of eponymous smartphones.

The Mirvishes

Honest Ed Mirvish (1914–2007) started out running a small store and eventually built it into the sprawling flamboyant Honest Ed's department store, replete with his name in thousands of flashing light bulbs. Then he branched out into live theatre, purchasing and restoring Toronto's Royal Alexandra Theatre, forming his own production company and becoming a generous philanthropist. His son David continues in his stead.

Simpsons

For decades, Simpsons and Eaton's were the Macy's and Gimbles of Canada—competing retail giants. As a distinctly Canadian retailer, Simpsons, though now long gone, is a happy reminder of Canada's long and often inadvertent path to forming its own national character.

Loblaws

This distinctly Canadian grocery store (the first location opened in 1919 in Toronto) has a name that, while mundane to our ears, sounds to newcomers like "Blah Blahs." A friend of mine used to go to trade shows and introduce himself thus: "Hi, I'm Rob Loblaw, Bob Loblaw's son." If you don't see why this is funny, try saying it out loud.

FAMILY FAME AND FORTUNE

Aspers

Movers and shakers in media ownership, the Aspers were owners of the now defunct CanWest Global TV network and briefly, the *National Post* newspaper.

Bronfmans

Starting out as ambitious and successful bootleggers, the Bronfmans were the owners of Seagram's Whiskey. Since then, the enormously wealthy Bronfman family has moved into other highly lucrative areas as well as becoming ardent philanthropists.

Eatons

Starting with patriarch Timothy Eaton (1834–1907) and continuing for the next couple of generations, the Eatons were Canada's retail royalty, operating the famous Eaton's department stores. The Eaton's mail-order catalogue brought the luxuries of the city to the country, and at the height of the Eaton empire, you could order an entire house (for example, Alberta's Neils Hogenson House, built in 1917) that was delivered in kit form. Although the Eaton's chain went bankrupt in 1999, the current generation of Eatons is still plenty rich.

Irvings

Starting with K.C. Irving (1899–1992), the Irvings built their empire in media, food processing, engineering, transport, construction and building supplies. All of these businesses were vertically integrated to supply one another's needs so that profits stayed within the company. Years ahead of their time and able to move quickly, since their businesses are still privately owned, the Irvings are worth billions.

Masseys

Starting out as blacksmiths in 1847, the Masseys eventually became the most prominent manufacturers of agricultural equipment in the Commonwealth of the United Kingdom. The Masseys were also generous philanthropists, building Toronto's Massey Hall and the University of Toronto's Massey College.

Reitmans

Take your pick—there are the Reitmans who are clothiers, running their eponymous chain of women's clothing stores (as well as Penningtons and AdditionElle) and the showbiz father and son, Ivan and Jason Reitman. As far as we know, the two families are not related.

Rogers

Ted Rogers Sr. (1900–39) invented the first radio receivers to run on household alternating current instead of large and inconvenient batteries. He subsequently founded radio station CFRB (Canada's First Rogers Batteryless). His son, Ted Rogers Jr. (1933–2008), built the Rogers media empire, starting first with cable TV, but then moving into telephony and Internet services as well.

Thomsons

Starting with Roy Thomson, 1st Baron Thomson of Fleet (1894–1976), who was a newspaper tycoon, the Thomsons have emerged as one of the richest families in Canada, with subsequent generations also becoming patrons of the arts.

BORED? INVENT A BOARD GAME

Never mind hockey, Canadians are also good at coming up with some of the world's favourite board games. If it's a rainy day at the cottage and you find yourself around the family table answering questions or making up outrageous definitions for words that may not exist or drawing pictures to represent words that do, you may have a Canadian to thank for it.

Balderdash

Invented by an actress and an ad man from Toronto, Balderdash sees players trying to fool one another into believing false definitions made up to describe real things.

Pictionary

This game, in which players try to guess words based on their teammates' presumably hilarious drawings intended as clues, has its roots north of the 49th parallel.

Trivial Pursuit

Since its development by two Canadians in the early 1980s, Trivial Pursuit has sold millions of games and filled countless heads with soon-forgotten knowledge.

Yahtzee

The U.S. developer of this game of dice-rolling bought the rights from a Canadian couple who, according to legend, came up with the idea on their yacht.

MOVING AND GROOVING

Yes, here you will find all the achingly obvious and obligatory sports (no less awesome for their obviousness and obligato), but to keep it interesting, I've tried to include feats of physical endurance that you might not immediately think of.

Alexander Mackenzie Paddles to the Arctic

Frankly, this early feat is so ridiculous I don't know why it isn't more famous. Never mind that Mackenzie beat Lewis and Clark to the Pacific Ocean by 10 years, but before he did that, he (and several hired minions) *paddled* in *birchbark canoes* from Lake Athabasca to the freakin' Arctic where they saw ice and whales. Then they came back. The round trip covered 5000 kilometres in about 100 days. *And* he did it by mistake, since he was actually looking for a route to the Pacific. Today, the river he paddled down, the longest in Canada at approximately 1735 kilometres, is named after him.

Basketball

This one's a bit dubious because the game's inventor, Dr. James Naismith, was something called a "Canadian American" (whatever the heck that means). While working at a YMCA in Springfield, Massachusetts, in 1891, Naismith was looking for a way to let his male secretarial students burn off some energy on foul-weather days, so he nailed up a couple of peach baskets at either end of the gym, gave his students a ball and history was made.

Blanket Toss

This traditional Inuit activity is somehow emblematically Canadian because it involves a group taking turns at working together to provide enjoyment to one of their number.

Right-wingers would call it "socialism," but sane people call it jointly grasping the edge of a blanket and using it to fling a member of your group as high as 6 metres into the air (like a trampoline). The blanket toss may have originated to let hunters spot faraway caribou herds or other prey.

Calgary Stampeders

Like Vancouver (see "Vancouver Grizzlies," p. 166), the city of Calgary has the good sense to give its teams names that make sense. Calgary's CFL team takes its name from the Calgary Stampede, but the name also suggests an unstoppable force trampling everything that stands in its way—what better sort of name for a CFL team?

Canadian Football

Our game has more players than in American football (12 vs. 11), a wider field and fewer downs. Is this, or is this not, a recipe for awesome?

Curling

Canadians love their curling. Something about the notion of sliding a heavy stone across some dimpled ice so it can crash into other heavy stones acts as a siren call on our psyches. Either that or our long, cold winters mean that we find just about anything interesting.

Dogsledding

There is possibly nothing finer than listening to the runners of your sled on the snow beneath as you watch the bouncing furry tails of your dog team pulling you smoothly across a frozen lake.

Five-pin Bowling

It's true—five-pin bowling was invented in Canada. Toronto bowling alley owner Tom Ryan removed half the pins and made the ball smaller either to accommodate patrons who found the 10-pin ball too heavy *or* to reduce the noise generated by falling pins that prevented customers from hearing the live band he provided—or both.

Hockey

Did the game stem from lacrosse or from scooting frozen cow patties around on frozen ponds with wooden sticks? Who cares? Your enjoyment of Canada's official winter sport will be in no way increased by my going on about it for pages and pages—other people have already done that.

Lacrosse

If you've ever watched a game of lacrosse, you know that it moves fast, with the exciting potential for broken bones and fights. Today this game, created by the Iroquois and appropriated by the French, is Canada's official summer sport.

Luge

It doesn't get any more awesome (or Canadian) than lying down on a little sled and zipping feet-first down a curving, icy tube at speeds of up to 140 kilometres per hour.

Montréal Canadiens

The "H" in the logo stands for "hockey," not "habitants," but this misnomer has become a happy bit of nicknaming for the "Habs," Montréal's much-beloved NHL team.

Montréal Expos

Named after the 1967 World's Fair held in Montréal, the Expos were the first Major League Baseball franchise to be awarded outside the U.S. In 2004, in a move that had absolutely *nothing* to do with money, the franchise was moved to Washington and renamed the Nationals.

Mountain Climbing

There's nothing like climbing a mountain. Not rock climbing, mind you; I'm talking about hiking up a steep slope and arriving at the top several hours later, tired and out of breath. Best feeling in the world. Canada has quite a few mountains, so you should give it a shot if you can.

One-legged Skater

Norman Falkner of Saskatoon lost a leg in World War I, but this avid skater was not to be put off. He developed a one-legged skating technique that, although he required a push at the beginning, was truly a wonder to behold.

ParticipACTION

This on-again off-again campaign to promote physical fitness takes the form of TV public service announcements, a web presence and occasional signage. For many people, the program's earliest incarnation brings to mind nostalgic memories of Canada in the 1970s and good-hearted memories of the 1990s, by which time ParticipACTION had shrivelled to a series of TV spots called "Body Break."

Québec Nordiques

Alas, they are no more, but the Nordiques were Québec City's storied NHL team from 1979 to 1995. Then the franchise was moved to…Colorado, because professional hockey is *not* all about money.

Skating

Not only is skating a delightful activity on its own, but it is also at the root of hockey.

Skiing

Whether it's cross-country or downhill, skiing provides countless moments of calm as well as Zen reflection mixed with instances of exhilaration and pure adrenaline.

Steppy-cock

You would hope that this Atlantic Canadian children's game has been declared illegal, consisting as it does of following the leader in a merry romp across *chunks of ice floating in the ocean.*

Toronto Blue Jays

Any baseball team that wins the World Series two years in a row (1992 and 1993) needs no further proof of its awesomeness.

Toronto Maple Leafs

Just kidding.

Vancouver Grizzlies

Vancouver's NBA team has a name that undeniably makes sense, since there are grizzly bears in BC and, from what I understand, they are ferocious players of basketball. I am perhaps unduly sensitive about the names of sports teams because of the Toronto

Raptors, the name of which makes me embarrassed to be from Toronto, because it lends credence to the notion that many of us are weak in the head. Why didn't we just call the team the *Toronto Jurassic Park*?

Powers That Be: "What shall we call our new basketball team?"

Torontonians: "Omigod, there's like this movie that came out this year, like, all about dinosaurs? And there were these dinosaurs we'd never heard of before called 'raptors,' and they were really cool and so now, like, everyone knows what raptors are and so, like, let's call our team the Toronto Raptors, because, like, there was this movie? And it was all about dinosaurs? And they were called raptors?"

I mean, geez Louise.

Women's Hockey League

In a typically progressive fashion, Canada has a professional women's hockey league, which, though still struggling to build an audience, is surely destined for greatness.

RACES AND OTHER COMPETITIONS

Bathtub Races

The month of May sees the annual bathtub races, covering the 782 kilometres between Whitehorse and Dawson. Hardy Yukoners hop in their "bathtubs" (watercraft that really only need to roughly conform to the approximate shape and dimensions of a bathtub rather than be an actual bathtub) and frantically (or lackadaisically, as the case may be) paddle over rapids, rough waters and strong currents toward the finish line.

Bluenose

Familiar to all as the tiny ship on our dime, the *Bluenose* was not only a working fishing schooner, but was also famous as a race-winning speedster of the eastern seaboard, suffering only one defeat in 17 years of racing, between 1921 and 1938.

Canada's Cup

Starting in 1896, this cross-border sailing race pitted Canadian and American challengers against one another. Since 2001, race participants have to use identical craft so that the emphasis is on sailing skills rather than boat design.

Canadian Challenge Dogsled Race

Since 1994, this annual race in Saskatchewan sees dogsled teams from around the world compete for the best time on the 600-kilometre track between Prince Albert and La Ronge. Adorably, the intrepid huskies wear Gore-Tex booties to protect their paws.

Fest du Voyageur

This 10-day winter festival is held in Winnipeg to celebrate the hardiness and *joi de vivre* of the voyageurs, the hard-paddling men on whose shoulders the fur trade was built.

Grey Cup

The battle for Canada's ultimate prize in professional football has been thrilling fans since it was first fought for in 1912 at the behest of Canada's ninth Governor General, the 4th Earl Grey, a relative of the 1st Earl Grey, for whom the eponymous tea is named.

Highland Games

All of the western, central and eastern provinces have highland games, with a particular celebrated round of games held each year in Antigonish, Nova Scotia, since 1863. If you're in the mood for caber tossing, stone putting and hammer throwing (not to mention great Celtic music and dancing), then hitch up your kilt and say, "Hoot mahn!"

King and Queen Trapper Competitions

These boisterous events, held in northern communities all across Canada, test contestants' skills at such tasks as log tossing, log splitting, axe throwing, tea boiling, leg wrestling, nail driving, bannock baking, snowshoeing and moose calling.

Logging Bees

Initially concerted, co-operative efforts to clear trees from a parcel of land, logging bees soon turned into wild celebrations of lumberjack skills such as clambering to the top of a tree and performing any number of outrageous feats with axes—sort of a highland games for loggers.

Mighty Man Competition

Held as one of the many events at Morden, Manitoba's annual Corn and Apple Festival, the Mighty Man Competition sees its undoubtedly strong contestants compete at a timed obstacle course called the Medley, which includes carrying a pair of 82-kilogram cylinders over a predetermined path, called the Farmer's Walk; pulling everyone's favourite piece of farm equipment for 24 metres by hand in the Tractor Pull; carrying a 227-kilogram pole in the Circle of Pain; and seeing who can hold up one end of a Pontiac Grand Am the longest in the aptly named Car Deadlift.

Pumpkin Regatta

Every year, Windsor, Nova Scotia, hosts its annual Pumpkin Regatta. Incredibly, the Great Pumpkin Race is exactly what the title suggests—eager contestants climb into giant hollowed-out pumpkins (for real) and paddle their way into history.

Smoke Show

You can't exactly call it exercise, but frankly, anything that gets Canadians away from their keyboards or game consoles is fair game as far as I'm concerned. Quiet-loving residents of Gronlid,

Saskatchewan, no doubt plug their ears for the annual spring tire-squealing contest.

Stanley Cup

Lord Stanley of Preston, Canada's sixth and seventh Governor General, was a big hockey fan. Around 1892, he bought a silver *punchbowl* and declared it the supreme prize for hockey playing in Canada. It was first awarded in 1893. Over the years, a replica punchbowl was created and placed upon a huge base to accommodate the names of each year's winners.

World Bunnock Championships

Not to be confused with the dense bread known as *bannock*, bunnock is a game played with horse ankle bones. Each year, 300 teams from as far away as Australia and Japan descend on Macklin, Saskatchewan, to compete. Macklin also boasts the World's Biggest Bunnock, a nearly 10-metre tall statue of a horse's ankle bone that bears a striking resemblance to a female mannequin torso with no limbs but a modest pair of art deco–style breasts.

IMPRESSIVE ATHLETICISM OR ACCOMPLISHMENT

Cutting the Border

Believe it or not, back in the late 19th century, a hardy band of loggers (well, several bands of hardy loggers) had to cut a slender ribbon of cleared land across the entire nation so that the border between the U.S. and Canada would always be clear—all 5525 kilometres of it.

Edmonton Grads

The Edmonton Grads were an all-female high school basketball team who still hold the record as North America's winningest sports team. Their full name was the Commercial Graduates Basketball team, representing, as they did, Edmonton's McDougall Commercial High School. Between 1915 and 1940, the team scored 502 victories against 20 losses, winning 93 percent of their games and taking 49 out of 51 domestic championships. Although women's basketball was not recognized as an Olympic sport until 1976, the Grads played several games in conjunction with the Olympics, winning all 27 of the games they played between 1924 and 1936. They were the world champions for 17 straight years. J.R. Naismith, the inventor of basketball, called them the "finest basketball team that ever stepped out on a floor."

1972 Summit Series

Pitting Russian and Canadian hockey teams against one another, the series was tied until Paul Henderson scored his dramatic overtime goal against the Russians to produce one of Canada's most enduring memories (and accompanying photograph).

Joshua Slocum (1844–1909)

Born and raised in Nova Scotia, Slocum ran away to sea in his
early teens, eventually settling in the U.S. Between 1895 and 1898,
Slocum became the first person to circumnavigate the earth
alone. His vessel for this historic undertaking was *Spray*, a gaff-
rigged sloop just over 11 metres long. Upon his return, he
penned a bestseller called *Sailing Alone Around the World*.
Slocum disappeared on a 1909 voyage and was presumed lost
at sea.

MAKING (AIR) WAVES

TV. Film. Music. Radio. Animation. Media theory. Media innovation. Canada is awesome because of so many different people, works and areas of media and entertainment that any list thereof must perforce be incomplete. Nonetheless, here's a friendly stab.

Canadian Broadcasting Corporation (CBC)

Canada's public broadcaster has been long renowned as a source of groundbreaking efforts in documentary journalism in radio, TV and now interactive. The radio arm especially is regarded as a unifying force in the mid-20th century. The Ceeb's attempts at dramatic and comedic entertainment have met with mixed success to say the least, yielding shows that are often regarded with a corny sort of nostalgia following their usually long-overdue cancellation.

Hollywood North

Since the mid-1980s, Toronto, Vancouver and now other areas across Canada have come to be known by this friendly nickname for their perennial popularity as film and TV locations (not to mention studio facilities, post-production houses and special-effects studios).

Nelvana

Named after early Canadian female superhero Nelvana of the Northern Lights (see p. 64), this studio and production company has been at the forefront of Canada's animation industry for more than three decades.

Treehouse

This cable TV outlet is recognized for its hugely popular and innovative children's programming.

Great Documentaries

Whether it's the National Film Board (see below), the CBC or an
upstart independent producer, Canadians have gained a worldwide
reputation as creative tellers of true stories.

National Film Board

As well as producing groundbreaking full-length documentaries,
the NFB is famous for its quirky, artfully executed animation
and charming live-action short subjects (or combinations thereof).
Some well-known NFB "vignettes" are *The Cat Came Back* and
The Log Driver's Waltz.

AWESOMELY ENTERTAINING PEOPLE

Marie Dressler (1868–1934)

Silent film star and comedienne who made the transition to talkies, winning an Oscar for the 1930 comedy/drama, *Min and Bill*. She played a similar role in 1933's famous *Tugboat Annie*.

Mack Sennet (1880–1960)

Silent film producer and director. Founded Keystone Studios. Invented the zany, madcap style of physical comedy that came to define early silent movies. Hired Charlie Chaplin.

Louis B. Mayer (1884–1957)

Founder of MGM (Metro Goldwyn Mayer) and creator of the "star system," Mayer was born in present-day Belarus, migrated to America and was raised in Saint John, New Brunswick, for a few years.

Mary Pickford (1892–1979)

Silent screen superstar. Co-founder of United Artists, along with Charlie Chaplin. D.W. Griffiths and Douglas Fairbanks. Known as "America's Sweetheart."

Norma Shearer (1902–83)

Actress famous for playing a "liberated woman" before the term existed. One biographer described her as the first "actress to make it chic and acceptable to be single and not a virgin on screen." She was also married to Hollywood legend Irving Thalberg.

John Drainie (1916–66)

Actor famous for portraying another great Canadian, Stephen Leacock. Orson Welles called him "the greatest radio actor in the world."

Shirley Douglas (b. 1934)

Mainstay actress on Canadian television. Daughter of the "father of Medicare," Tommy Douglas. Mother of Kiefer Sutherland.

Donald Sutherland (b. 1935)

Actor excelling at offbeat but wholly believable characterizations. His roles are so many and so varied that to list them all would severely jeopardize the possibility of including anything else in this book.

Ryan Larkin (1943–2007)

Animator famous for the 1969 short *Walking*, which was nominated for an Oscar.

Tom Jackson (b. 1948)

Métis actor who has appeared on *North of Sixty*, *Shining Time Station* and *Star Trek: The Next Generation*. Jackson also produced of a series of annual charity Christmas concerts called Huron Carole.

Des McAnuff (b. 1952).

Director of Broadway musicals and artistic director of the Stratford Festival.

Graham Greene (b. 1952)

Not to be confused with the English novelist of the same name, Greene is an actor of First Nations heritage, recognizable for his roles in the TV series *Northern Exposure* and *Red Green*, as well as film roles in *Die Hard with a Vengeance*, *Thunderheart* and *Twilight: New Moon*.

Les Stroud (b. 1961)

Better known as the star of *Survivorman*, Stroud is a survivalist who uses his wits to survive in the wild for a week or more, filming himself all the way. He also plays a mean blues harmonica.

Mike Holmes (b. 1963)

Everyone's favourite handyman hunk hosts, among others, *Holmes on Homes* and *Holmes Inspection*. He has also authored two books and is actively involved in various charitable foundations.

Kiefer Sutherland (b. 1966)

Actor and son of Shirley Douglas and Donald Sutherland, which makes him Tommy Douglas' grandson. Most famous for playing Jack Bauer in the hit TV series *24*.

Nathan Fillion (b. 1971)

Actor, most notably in Joss Whedon's short-lived but beloved *Firefly* TV series and later, the ABC network mystery series *Castle*.

Ryan Reynolds (b. 1976)

Actor, Hollywood star. Film credits include *Blade: Trinity*, *X-Men Origins: Wolverine* and *Green Lantern*.

Rachel McAdams (b. 1978)

Actress in such films as *Mean Girls*, *The Notebook*, *Wedding Crashers*, *Sherlock Holmes* and the sequel, *Sherlock Holmes: A Game of Shadows*.

Ryan Gosling (b. 1980)

Actor and Hollywood heartthrob in such movies as *The Notebook* but also with a reputation for standout performances in grittier fare like *Blue Valentine* and the offbeat romance *Lars and the Real Girl*.

Michael Cera (b. 1988)

Actor who plays self-aware geek extraordinaire. Films include *Juno, Super Bad, Youth in Revolt* and *Scott Pilgrim vs. the World*, the last being remarkable for actually being set (not merely filmed) in Toronto.

ASSORTED ENTERTAINMENT AWESOMENESS

As It Happens (CBC Radio)

The CBC's "reverse call-in" radio show has been phoning anywhere in the world there is news since 1968. AIH is an amazing mixture of serious news stories (interviewing an African woman whose door was broken down by murderous rebels while on the air) to the lighthearted and whimsical (an ongoing community dispute in England regarding a large fibreglass fish), as well as delineating places as being a certain number of miles from the small English village of Reading.

The Cat Came Back (NFB)

This 1988 animated musical short about a man who can't get rid of a destructive cat entered the national consciousness as one of the NFB's many fine interstitials, shown in otherwise unfilled gaps of TV air time.

Degrassi (CBC/CTV/MuchMusic)

This wildly popular and long-lasting franchise now comprises multiple series and properties: *The Kids of Degrassi Street* (1979–86), *Degrassi Junior High* (1987–89), *Degrassi High* (1989–91) and *Degrassi: The Next Generation* (2001–).

Mr. Dressup (CBC)

From 1967 to 1996 and for more than 4000 episodes, Ernie Coombs (1927–2001) played the avuncular Mr. Dressup, who led his young audience through simple crafts, told stories, dressed up with costumes from the Tickle Trunk and played surrogate parent to two puppets named Casey and Finnegan (a small, androgynous child and a dog, respectively).

Due South (various networks)

From 1994 to 1999, this comedy-mystery featured a polite and highly competent Mountie (Paul Gross) improbably teamed with a less polite but highly enthusiastic Chicago police detective (played first by David Marciano and then Callum Keith Rennie).

Friendly Giant (CBC)

Friendly Giant (his name was "Friendly") was portrayed by Bob Homme in this long-running classic kids' series that featured stories, music and puppets, most notably Jerome the Giraffe and Rusty the Rooster. Over the course of 3000-plus episodes, it ran from 1958 to 1985.

Heritage Minutes (various networks)

Since the 1990s, these short interstitial re-enactments dramatized great moments in Canadian history and have been widely spoofed and satirized. One comedy troupe told the story of the Heritage Minute in the form of…a Heritage Minute.

Hockey Night in Canada (CBC)

Starting on radio and then moving to TV, HNIC (or as it is also known, "Hockey Fight in Canada") has been on the air in some form or another since 1931.

The Log Driver's Waltz (NFB)

This 1979 short combined a song of the same name set to live-action footage of log drivers leaping from log to log of a massive log boom. The live-action eventually morphs into whimsically delightful animation and then back again. Like *The Cat Came Back*, *The Log Driver's Waltz* occasionally popped up on TV in the 1970s and '80s as filler.

The Starlost (CTV)

Widely reviled as one of the worst science-fiction programs ever made, *The Starlost* lasted only one season (1973). Initially, it seemed to have promise, based on a concept developed by U.S. sci-fi super-star Harlan Ellison and with special effects by Hollywood legend Douglas Trumbull. Alas, after multiple budget cuts, network interference and the failure of Trumbull's patented "MagiCam System" (anything that involves two cameras, a green screen and a periscope is sure to be trouble), Ellison disowned any involvement and insisted upon being credited by the pseudonym Cordwainer Bird.

This Hour Has Seven Days (CBC)

From 1964 to 1966, this groundbreaking and often controversial news magazine–style TV program brought Canadians face to face with contentious topics of the day through ambush interview tactics, comedy sketches and all-round good reporting.

Quirks and Quarks (CBC Radio)

Since 1975, CBC Radio's popular and accessible weekend science show has brought listeners the answers to questions they might never have dreamed of before (or alternately that might have been knocking around in their heads for ages).

Space Command (CBC)

Over the course of two seasons from 1953 to 1954, *Space Command* served as one the CBC's earliest original children's programmes. Following the crew of an imaginary space station, the show was notable for appearances by Canadian actors James Doohan, who later played Scotty in *Star Trek*, and perhaps inevitably, Captain Kirk himself, William Shatner. Only one episode is known to survive.

Walking (NFB)

This 1968 five-minute film by animator Ryan Larkin is still shown in animation schools today as a classic study of different human gaits. It took Larkin two years to complete, partly because of his time-consuming ink-wash painting method.

CINEMA

Canadian movies are probably the best you've never seen. There isn't a big market for Canadian films (Québec is the exception to the rule), since we have less than 10 percent of the population of our neighbour to the south. Some of these movies you've probably never seen, but they may have influenced subsequent movies you probably also didn't see. I personally have only seen eight of the following movies, but I did see the SCTV spoof of Goin' Down the Road, *which might as well count as seeing the real thing, since that was how I found out about the film to begin with.*

Nanook of the North (1922)

Filmed by an American, the film follows the life of an Inuit family in northern Québec and is considered Canada's first feature-length documentary. A huge hit when released (in spite of the director dropping a cigarette on it and incinerating 30,000 feet of film), the film later drew criticism when it was discovered that many scenes had been staged.

Goin' Down the Road (1970)

This East Coast slang term for "going out of province to look for work" perfectly suits this story of two Maritimers who travel from economically depressed Nova Scotia to Toronto in search of good jobs and better lives. The movie was celebrated for its gritty realism and honest portrayal of the economic difficulties that were starting to dog eastern provinces.

Mon Oncle Antoine (1971)

Acclaimed as one of the greatest Canadian films ever made, the story follows a 15-year-old boy's coming of age in a rural of 1940s

Quebec, where the main industry is asbestos mining. It is a snap-shot of social and religious values just prior to the famous asbes-tos strike of 1949 and the social upheaval that followed decades later during the Quiet Revolution.

The Rowdy Man (1972)

Written by and starring Gordon Pinsent, this movie has been called one of the best films about East Coast life to come out of the 1970s. It follows the life of a boozing, brawling prankster who's out to have a good time with no regard for the consequences of his actions.

The Silent Partner (1978)

One of the few films to feature a soundtrack by Oscar Peterson, this suspense thriller stars Eliot Gould as the hero and Christopher Plummer as a psychotic shopping mall Santa Claus. My parents were thrilled when they saw this movie because the opening scene takes place on the escalators at the Eaton Centre in Toronto, and it was a novelty to see a film that was *set* in our city.

Porky's (1982)

Okay, the odds are that if you haven't seen this film, you've heard of it. This tale of teenagers who exact revenge after they are humil-iated in their quest for a prostitute is a progenitor of the gross-out movie. Although directed by an American and shot in Florida, *Porky's* was funded by Canada's Astral Media, meaning we have only ourselves to blame for fare like *American Pie*.

The Fly (1986)

Because mention of David Cronenberg is *de rigeur* in any discus-sion of Canadian cinema, I have opted for his remake of the 1958 film of the same name, which arguably exposed Cronenberg's oeuvre of bodily fluids, unnatural organs and intelligent gross-ness to a wider audience.

Jesus of Montréal (1989)

Sobering and inspirational all at once, the film tells the story of a controversial Passion play and the parallels between its production and the story of Christ. Perhaps it has to do with its timeless theme, but the film stands up very well today.

Roadkill (1989) and Highway 61 (1991)

I'm counting these Bruce McDonald movies as one film since they are really the same film done over again, but no less entertaining for it. Both feature naïve, slightly repressed wallflowers who find themselves by going on epic road trips during which they encounter copious amounts of rock 'n' roll as well as secondary characters who either (a) are aspiring serial killers, or (b) think they're Satan.

Exotica (1994)

Just when you thought you were going to get through this section without anything by Atom Egoyan, here it is. This disturbing but ultimately compassionate movie tells a complex story out of sequence, and it is only near the end of the film that we discover the shared event that has led so many of the broken characters to the points at which we meet them.

The Delicate Art of Parking (2003)

A mini modern masterpiece, this good-hearted mockumentary looks at the opinions and lives of parking enforcement personnel. It features Fred Ewanuick and Nancy Robertson who both went on to star in *Corner Gas*.

C.R.A.Z.Y. (2005)

Another Québec classic, this film tells the story of a young man growing up in Québec in the 1960s and '70s. His struggle to come out of the closet to his family is the backbone of the plot, but the sharply observed period references—the constant smoking and a mother who makes toast by squishing bread under an electric iron—form a wonderfully whimsical backdrop.

Bon Cop, Bad Cop (2006)

Nothing says Canada like hockey, pot and bilingual bickering, all three of which figure in this successful, self-consciously Canadian comedy. One of the film's highlights is the scene in which a secondary character expounds on the different ways that Francophones and Anglophones pronounce the word "tattoo."

Away From Her (2006)

Marking Canadian actress, director and screenwriter Sarah Polley's feature-length debut, this film follows the unravelling of a marriage as a result of Alzheimer's disease. It won many awards and was nominated for two Oscars.

ALL THE WORLD'S A STAGE

Canada enjoys a wealth of riches in the performing arts, and I've already touched on many of them in previous sections of this book, but here, for the record, are a few that were left over.

The Stratford Festival

Yes, Canada's largest Shakespearean festival is certainly awesome, but when you consider that when it began in the early 1950s, Stratford was little more than a backwoods agricultural community in southern Ontario that somehow attracted top-notch British talent back to the colonies, the whole tale becomes yet more awesome.

Bard on the Beach

Since 1990, Vancouver's resident Shakespeare company presents the Bard's classic works in full view of the sunset over the Pacific Ocean. Elizabethan theatre is seldom more beautiful.

Robert Lepage (b. 1957)

It may seem strange to include a person in a list that consists otherwise of companies, but Lepage's work as a theatrical director, characterized by innovative and often jaw-dropping staging techniques have set the bar for the creative mixture of live actors and multimedia production elements.

Cirque du Soleil

Founded in Québec in 1984 and famous the world over, le Cirque eschews animals, instead focusing on the amazing feats of its human gymnasts, dancers and performers. With each show telling a story, the company has so far produced 30 huge touring shows ranging in inspiration from simply "mystery" to the music of popular artists like The Beatles and Michael Jackson.

Opera Atelier

If all the other stuff in this list isn't highbrow enough for you, meet Opera Atelier. Canada's only baroque opera company mounts works from the 17th and 18th centuries in lush, gorgeously designed shows. Using period instrumentation and costumes, the company is also notable for sometimes presenting operas that are rarely performed live with such complete staging.

TV SHOWS

There's an old joke that goes like this:

Q: How many Canadians does it take to screw in a light bulb?

A: Four. One to screw in the light bulb and three to point and say, "He's Canadian!"

And, in many ways, this is the story of Canadians in comedy. We do just fine on our own (especially south of the border), but then, inevitably, someone comes along and goes, "Hey, you're a Canadian!" It could be a fellow Canuck or it could be a surprised American, but either way, the cat is now out of the bag. It never really makes a difference to the person's career, but now there is also a lingering, ghostly label; you're no longer just a comedian (successful or otherwise), now you're a Canadian. Then people forget, and you can once again go about your business of making them laugh.

Royal Canadian Air Farce (Radio 1973–97; TV 1980–2008)

In many ways this broad satire of Canadian politics and society modelled Canadian politics and society themselves—to some degree, fresh and irreverent, but later ossifying into a staid institution.

King of Kensington (1975–80)

Gently funny but socially conscious, the show starred Al Waxman as the owner of a convenience store in Toronto's ethnically diverse Kensington Market.

Saturday Night Live (1975–present)

This U.S. show was created by a Canadian (Lorne Michaels) and over the years has employed a rotating stable of Canadian talent: Dan Aykroyd, Martin Short, Mike Myers and assorted members of the comedy troupe Kids in the Hall.

SCTV (1976–84)

Typically avant-garde meta-comedy, *SCTV* took us through a condensed broadcast day on the fictional (and very low budget) SCTV network, allowing for satirical takes on real shows, people and television trends. Almost all the onscreen talent went on to become huge stars in the U.S. and Canada.

CODCO (1987–92)

This darkly funny sketch comedy show skewered East Coast politics with an ever-present taint of Catholicism floating disturbingly over the proceedings.

Kids in the Hall (1988–94)

Regarded by many as Canada's answer to Monty Python, not least for their inspired use of drag, surrealism and ruthless social commentary, Kids in the Hall (both the troupe itself and its eponymous TV show) were simply unlike anything before or after in both their unique outlook and commitment to "seeing it through."

The Red Green Show (1991–2006)

The fictional inhabitants of Possum Lodge, led by the eponymous Red Green, believed that if a man can't be handsome, he should be handy. This led to outrageous and usually unsuccessful ventures involving duct tape.

This Hour Has 22 Minutes (1993–present)

In some ways the logical heir to *CODCO* (originating on the East Coast and sharing various personnel), THH22M is a satirical news program (after *This Hour Has Seven Days*) that comments on real events with mordant wit and sly humour.

Corner Gas (2004–09)

There had been Canadian situation comedies before, but often the comedy was sorely missing. *Corner Gas* was an instant hit, following the lives of six citizens in fictional Dog River, Saskatchewan, with wit and affection. The town of Dog River was "portrayed" by the real town of Rouleau, Saskatchewan.

FUNNY FOLK

Stephen Leacock (1869–1944)

Possibly unique among humorists for being equally well known during his lifetime as a respected political theorist, Leacock can be seen in many ways as the progenitor of the "outsider" position that has come to characterize much of Canadian humour, despite Leacock himself being a somewhat xenophobic monarchist.

Wayne and Schuster

Johnny Wayne (1918–90) and Frank Schuster (1916–2002) were true pioneers of Canadian comedy. They found success on radio and TV, notably refusing to permanently move to the U.S., instead staying proudly Canadian.

Lorne Michaels (b. 1944)

Creator and producer of *Saturday Night Live* and producer of *Kids in the Hall*—that's enough awesome for anyone.

Dan Aykroyd (b. 1952)

Where to begin? Aykroyd originated several classic characters during the early seasons of *Saturday Night Live* and went on to start in movies left, right and centre, perhaps most memorably as Elwood Blues in *The Blues Brothers*, opposite fellow *SNL* alumnus John Belushi.

Mary Walsh (b. 1952)

The *This Hour Has 22 Minutes* alumna is perhaps best known for her occasionally dressed-like-a-Viking character Marg Delahunty, who ambushes political figures with the cameras rolling and does her best to lay bare their (circle one): Stupidity. Hypocrisy. Greed. Cluelessness. Willingness to go along with a joke.

Jim Carrey (b. 1962)

First finding fame on *In Living Color*, Carrey shot to movie stardom with *Ace Ventura: Pet Detective, Dumb and Dumber, The Mask, Liar Liar, The Truman Show* and *Man on the Moon* (among others).

Mike Myers (b. 1963)

Raised in Scarborough, Ontario (like many other brilliant Canadians), Myers rose to prominence when he was cast as a writer and performer on *Saturday Night Live*. He is probably most famous for his two characters, Wayne Campbell and Austin Powers, and their accompanying film series.

Will Ferguson (b. 1964)

The bestselling author of *Why I Hate Canadians, Beauty Tips from Moose Jaw* and other books affectionately looks askance at Canada. He won the 2012 Giller Prize for his book *419: A Novel*. He has also thrice won the Leacock Memorial Medal for Humour.

Dashan (b. 1965)

Born in Ottawa, Mark Rowswell is likely China's most famous foreign national under his stage name Dashan. Fluent in Mandarin, he became famous in part because of his exceptional abilities at Xiansheng, a form of "cross-talk" comedy delivered at high speeds and with extensive wordplay and puns.

Samantha Bee (b. 1969)

Samantha Bee has found fame (and probably a bit of fortune, too) as a regular correspondent on *The Daily Show* (when, as she herself acknowledges, she isn't busy being pregnant or giving birth).

Rick Mercer (b. 1969)

Another *This Hour Has 22 Minutes* alumnus, Mercer graduated to his own show, *The Rick Mercer Report.* He is perhaps best remembered for his "Talking to Americans" segments in which he would get Americans to agree to ridiculous statements about Canada, such as congratulating us for finally adopting the 24-hour clock.

Matthew Perry (b. 1969)

Famous to millions as Chandler Bing on *Friends*, Perry is (in part) from Ottawa.

Russell Peters (b. 1970)

This stand-up comedian of Anglo-Indian heritage regularly sells out stadiums and arenas around the world with his blend of affectionate, yet mocking humour targeting any and all cultural groups.

FESTIVITY EXTRA LARGE

Get ready for a wild ride through the topsy-turvy calendar of mass Canadian get-togethers. From the eccentric to the mainstream, public events and gatherings in Canada may be seasonal celebrations, expressions of whimsy or accidental traditions. Whatever their origins, you can rest assured that fun and convivial companionship await. Go!

Calgary Stampede

For 10 days in July, Cowtown puts on "The Greatest Outdoor Show on Earth" for more than one million visitors. There are rodeo competitions, chuckwagon races, First Nations exhibitions and, apparently, enough pancakes to collapse inward on themselves and create a black hole filled with syrup.

Canadian National Exhibition (CNE)

In Toronto, you know that fall is just around the corner when the Ex opens. It's a time to get in all the "summering" you may have missed, and there's nowhere better than the CNE, with rides, a midway, concerts and strangely trending unhealthy foods.

Carnaval de Québec

Québec City hosts the world's largest winter festival, which unfolds in early February and is instantly recognizable for its famous mascot, Monsieur Bonhomme, a big, plush snowman with a red sash. The impressive opening ceremonies take place in Bonhomme's ice palace and are followed by outdoor sports events (snowshoe and dogsled racing, among others), as well as the obligatory ice-sculpture contest.

Elvis Festival

Every July, Collingwood, Ontario, holds its annual Elvis Festival to celebrate Canada's greatest figure skater, Elvis Stojko. But, seriously, it celebrates Elvis Presley—all sorts of Elvis, from skinny to fat, young to old. There are even singing competitions. I can't confirm this, but I stubbornly believe that at one time, Collingwood held the world's record for the greatest number of parachuting Elvises. You'd think something like that would be listed on the official website—it's not, but frankly, having a legitimate reason to type the words "parachuting Elvises" isn't one that most writers get to have nearly often enough.

Expo '67

The 1967 World's Fair was held in Montréal and dubbed Expo '67. It happily fell during Canada's centennial year and is fondly remembered as a year of hard work (on the part of Montréalers to get ready) and then of seriously groovy vibes (enjoying the eyes of the world upon us) as Canada's future and possibilities seemed truly limitless.

Festival de la Tourbe

During the month of July, visitors to Lamèque, New Brunswick, may notice that homes and business are festively decorated with bales of peat moss (*la tourbe*). The reason for this is because the city hosts what may be the world's only festival celebrating the harvest of peat moss (the commercial applications of which, I fully confess, are unknown to me).

Festival des choux de Bruxelles

I maintain that Brussels sprouts are the gristle of the vegetable kingdom—lacking in visceral appeal and tough to chew. The inhabitants of Rogersville, New Brunswick, do not appear to share this sentiment, inexplicably staging an annual Brussels sprout festival at the end of July. As someone who thinks that Brussels sprouts are anti-awesome, the highlight to me sounds like a Brussels sprout battle that involves people whipping the little bruisers at each another with as much force as possible.

Maple Sugar Festivals

You'll find these all across the country, usually in the spring when the sap from maple trees starts to run. You'll get to sample maple candy, maple sugar and a surfeit of pancakes along with other vehicles for maple syrup. Usually there is also the comforting presence of cheesy souvenir vendors and all kinds of deliciously artery-clogging wursts and sausages. Having a maple leaf on our flag has never been more pleasing.

Oktoberfest

Held on or around Canadian Thanksgiving in Kitchener, Ontario, this nine-day festival is second only in size to the Oktoberfest in Germany. You will find a massive parade, oom-pah-pah bands, beer, delicious sausages, beer, fun activities for the kiddies, beer (not recommended for the kiddies) and, if I haven't already mentioned it, beer.

Pacific National Exhibition (PNE)

In many ways—in size, scale and approximate age—the PNE and the CNE are Pacific and Central siblings. While Vancouver's PNE is definitely West Coast in its sensibility, it too boasts crowds, rides, concerts and outlandish midway snack fare.

Royal Winter Fair

Initially started as a sort of "Agri-Con" for farmers and purveyors of farm equipment to gawk at one another, Toronto's enormously popular agricultural fair has today morphed into the only opportunity that kids born in the city may get to see cows and pigs. The mainstays of livestock prizes, shiny new tractors and butter sculptures happily continue.

Sunflower Festival

Okay, compared to the Brussels sprout festival (see above), this is a festival I can totally get behind. Sunflowers are tall, cheery and yellow, with an appealing circle of brown seeds in the middle—also, unlike Brussels sprouts, your parents are unlikely to boil them and expect you to ingest them without throwing up. Oh, right, back to the sunflower festival. It has been held every July since 1964 in Altona, Manitoba, which bills itself as "The Sunflower Capital of the World." Since sunflowers lack the projectile inertia of Brussels sprouts, the highlight of the festival is probably the crowning of the Sunflower Queen (who wins a trip to, for some unexplained reason, Australia).

Toonik Tyme

Held in Iqaluit (formerly Frobisher Bay), Toonik Tyme welcomes the spring thaw after months of cold winter. The festival presents aspects of traditional and modern Inuit life; for example, igloo building and snowmobile racing. The Tuniq were a culture who inhabited the Arctic before the Inuit and were dubbed "Paleo Eskimos" by archaeologists in a time before political correctness.

Winterlude

Over the course of three weekends in February, Gatineau, Québec, and Ottawa, Ontario, share the happy burden of hosting this huge festival featuring ice sculptures, slides, rides, skating and a general celebration of all things winter. It is a welcome respite from the winter blahs.

Zombie Walks

Canadians cannot lay claim to the invention of this phenomenon, but we were early adopters. The world's first zombie walk was held in 2001 in Sacramento, California, but Canada soon followed with the second in Toronto in 2003. For those unfamiliar with this activity, it involves dressing up en masse like zombies and staggering through some downtown area, often with the ultimate destination being a bar.

FRIENDLY REMINDERS

We see them in big, fuzzy costumes at sporting events. We purchase them from cheesy souvenir shops. They teach students about health and traffic safety. They rally our patriotic fervour in times of war. These are Canada's mascots.

Big Joe Mufferaw

There really was a Big Joe Mufferaw—he was a French Canadian lumberjack, strongman and boxer named Joseph Montferrand who lived from 1802 to 1864. Although he was quite well known during his lifetime, after his death, he was immortalized in legend, his name being anglicized to "Mufferaw." He may be the inspiration for the Paul Bunyan character who almost certainly derives from a French Canadian folklore character called "Paul Bonyenne." Big Joe Mufferaw is probably best remembered today through being fêted in a song of the same name by Stompin' Tom.

Elmer the Safety Elephant

Created in 1947 after the mayor of Toronto saw a similar program in Detroit, Elmer teaches children the rules of road safety for pedestrians. After Toronto saw a 44-percent drop in children being struck by vehicles, Elmer became the spearhead of a national program. I remember seeing Elmer on a cheery green flag fluttering from my school's flagpole, a friendly reminder to be safe as I crossed the road.

Jean Baptiste

This personification of French-speaking Canada is more "all purpose" than Johnny Canuck and is often portrayed wearing a jolly blue or red stocking cap.

Johnny Canuck

This personification of English-speaking Canada has appeared variously as a soldier, a lumberjack and a superhero. First created in the 1880s to represent Canada in relation to the U.S. in political cartoons of the day, during World War II, Johnny morphed into a Canadian superhero who helped fight Nazis.

Monsieur Bonhomme

The mascot of Québec's Carnaval is a big, fuzzy snowman that opens and closes the ceremony as well as walking about during the winter festival. Although his name translates literally as "good man," it can also be seen as a play on "bonhomie," or convivial companionship.

Murphy the Molar

Introduced by the Government of Ontario in the 1970s, Murphy was a talking molar whose roots were his feet and who also had arms, nose and eyes. He promoted good dental hygiene practices. Did other provinces have dental mascots, too? I've tried to find out, but alas, to no avail.

Peter Puck

Also known as the "Irrepressible Imp of the Ice," Peter is a walking, talking puck that explains the rules of hockey. First created in the 1970s, the character has had something of a resurgence in recent years.

HEAR THEM ROAR

Remarkable Canadian women (they are all remarkable in my opinion) have been listed extensively throughout this book, but, not surprisingly, there are more.

Rose Fortune (1774–1864)

Rose Fortune is often credited as Canada's first black police woman, which she undoubtedly was, albeit self-appointed. She started out as a luggage porter for passengers arriving by boat to Annapolis Royal, Nova Scotia. When gangs of ne'er-do-well boys began harassing her clients, and Rose herself, she promptly imposed a curfew at the docks and could be counted upon to dispatch miscreants by whacking them with a stick. Rose also started a cartage company that her family ran until 1980. In 1984, one of Rose's descendants, Daurene Lewis, was elected mayor of Annapolis, making her Canada's first black female mayor.

Emily Stowe (1831–1903)

Canada's first woman doctor had to go to the U.S. for training, since no Canadian medical school would take her. Stowe had the last laugh, though, when her daughter Augusta Stowe became the first woman to graduate from a Canadian medical school in 1883.

Emma Albani (1847–1930)

The Celine Dion of her day, Emma Albani was the first Canadian singer to achieve international stardom. A soprano, she sang the world's greatest opera roles all over the world, and she was once greeted by a crowd of 10,000 fans when she arrived for a concert in Montréal.

The Valiant Five

These five women launched the infamous "Persons Case" that convinced Canadian lawmakers to recognize women as "persons qualified to vote." They were Nellie McClung (1873–1951), also famous as an author; Henrietta Muir Edwards (1849–1931); Emily Murphy (1868–1933), also well known for being the first female magistrate in the British Empire; Louise McKinney (1868–1931), the first woman elected to the Legislative Assembly of Alberta); and Irene Parlby (1868–1965), the first female cabinet minister in Alberta.

Rosemary Brown (1930–2003)

In 1972, Rosemary Brown was elected to the Legislative Assembly of British Columbia. This made her the first black woman to be elected to a political office in Canada.

Naomi Klein (b. 1970)

This author and activist is best known as a critic of corporate globalization and the war in Iraq. Her books are *No Logo, Fences and Windows, The Take* and *The Shock Doctrine.*

PLANES, TRAINS AND SNOW MACHINES

It's hardly surprising in a country with so much empty space separating its inhabitants that getting around (and so, closer together) has long been a going concern. Suffice it to say, we have some unique modes of transport in Canada. No, not just dogsleds and snowmobiles (although those are good, too), but other more mundane modes of awesomely Canadian locomotion.

Gimli Glider

On July 23, 1983, a Boeing 767 Air Canada passenger jet ran out of fuel in midair because of a recent equipment conversion from imperial to metric. When the engines failed over Manitoba, with 61 passengers and eight crew members aboard, pilot Robert Pearson knew that his flight would never make it to Edmonton. With multiple simultaneous equipment failures, Pearson, also a qualified glider pilot, managed to land the massive jet on an abandoned military runway near Gimli, Manitoba. There were no serious injuries to the passengers or crew or to any of the spectators at a drag race that was taking place on the old runway. The entire amazing incident came to be referred to simply as the Gimli Glider.

Silver Dart

Although fabricated in the U.S., the Silver Dart became the first aircraft to fly in Canada, in 1909, at Baddeck, Nova Scotia. It was designed in part by Alexander Graham Bell, who maintained a residence in Baddeck. When two people flew in it at one time, it also marked the first passenger flight in Canada.

Kettle Valley Steam Railway

"Heritage railways" are dotted all across Canada, usually featuring a working steam locomotive. A shining example is the Kettle Valley Steam Railway (KVSR), featuring the 100-year-old locomotive, #3716. Running its route near Summerland, BC, the KVSR takes passengers on a 90-minute journey back through time, passing 70 metres over the Trout Creek Valley on a restored wooden trestle bridge.

Saskatchewan Western Development Museum (Moose Jaw branch)

There are four of these museums scattered across Saskatchewan, each showcasing a different theme. In Yorkton, it's "Story of People"; in Saskatoon, the museum is themed "1910 Boomtown"; in North Battleford, it's formatted as a "Heritage Farm and Village"; and in Moose Jaw, it is "History of Transportation." Inside the massive, sprawling Moose Jaw branch, you will find locomotives, streetcars, buses, cars and even airplanes. Sometimes these modes of transportation are set in full-scale mock-ups of streets, train stations and garages. It's a truly amazing experience and great for the kids.

Samuel Cunard (1787–1865)

Born in Halifax, Nova Scotia, Cunard was a born entrepreneur, managing his own general store at the age of 17 and later building the massive fleet of prestigious and profitable passenger steamships for which he is best remembered today. Cunard Steamships Limited eventually became so successful that they absorbed several other steamship companies, including the White Star Line, owners of the *Titanic*.

Ski-Doo

Comparatively few countries can claim to have invented a specific mode of transportation, and Canada is a member of this elite group. When J.A. Bombardier introduced the first Ski-Doo in 1959, he originally wanted to call it the "Ski-Dog" to suggest that it was taking over from dogsled teams. However, when a printer misread Bombardier's handwriting, possibly associating it with the early 20th-century catchphrase, "23 skiddoo," the vehicle's name became, instead, the famous Ski-Doo brand.

Tundra Buggy

If you ever find yourself in Churchill, Manitoba, be sure to book a ride on the Tundra Buggy. This big-wheeled behemoth is the only safe way to see polar bears in their natural habitat and with some degree of bumpy comfort.

THE MAPLE LEAF
IN ORBIT

Alouette 1

Launched in 1962, *Alouette* was Canada's first satellite. Although NASA launched *Alouette*, it was the first satellite constructed by a country other than the U.S. or the USSR. It was named for the French Canadian folk song "Alouette" (*alouette* is French for "skylark").

Anik

The Anik series of satellites (1972–2007) was named for an Inuktitut word meaning "brother." There were eight Aniks, each lobbed into orbit for Telesat Canada to boost television broadcast capability in Canada.

The CanadArm

Canada's most famous (and only) appendage in space, the CanadArm first saw service on the space shuttle *Columbia* in 1981, with a CanadArm in use on each of the shuttles until the retirement of the shuttle fleet in 2011. Also known as the Shuttle Remote Manipulator System (SRMS), the CanadArm was a 15-metre-long, elbowed robotic arm with a swivelling grasping mechanism at the end.

Mark Garneau (b. 1949)

The first Canadian in space, Garneau flew on three different shuttle missions—once on *Challenger* and twice on *Endeavour*.

Bob Thirsk (b. 1953)

At the time of writing this book, Thirsk has spent more time in space than any other Canadian—204 days, 18 hours. Julie Payette, after arriving at the International Space Station in July 2009, greeted Thirsk, which made them the first two Canadians to meet in space.

Chris Hadfield (b. 1959)

Hadfield was the first Canadian to walk in space, and in December 2012, he became the first Canadian to command the International Space Station.

Julie Payette (b. 1963)

Payette flew two missions, first on *Discovery* and again on *Endeavour*, both of which docked with the International Space Station.

MINDS THAT MATTER

We've had, and continue to have, bumper crops of big brains in Canada, federal politics notwithstanding. Note the striking absence of politicians on the list below. Anyway, the five people who follow are not the sum total of our grey-matter giants, but they do offer a good cross-section of disciplines and, in many cases, some of Canada's heavy thinkers are covered elsewhere in this book.

Marshall McLuhan (1911–80)

The man who coined the phrase "The media is the message" was arguably the most influential media theorist of the mid-to-late 20th century. He is also widely credited with "predicting" the advent of the World Wide Web nearly 30 years before it came to be. His notion that the advent of "new media" could help us to deepen interactions *with one another* now seems somewhat optimistic.

Northrop Frye (1912–91)

Seen by some as the foremost literary critic of the 20th century, Frye redefined the way that people write about writing. He was also likely the first to assess early Canadian literature and to arrive at the conclusion that it was shaped by nature and Canadians' sometimes uneasy relationship to it.

Jane Jacobs (1916–2006)

This American ex-pat living in Canada was a key writer and theorist on the role of cities in the lives of their residents and their impact on the fabric of society. While living in New York in the 1950s and '60s, she spearheaded an ultimately successful movement to prevent Washington Square Park from being obliterated by the proposed Lower Manhattan Expressway. Later, in Toronto, she was also instrumental in halting the proposed Spadina Expressway, to the immense relief of residents and taxpayers.

John Polyani (b. 1929)

Co-recipient of the 1986 Nobel Prize in Chemistry for his work in using infrared chemiluminescence (chemicals that glow) to observe how energy disperses during chemical reactions. To attempt to summarize it any more than this would seem to suggest that I understand it.

Frank Gehry (b. 1929)

Gehry is famous the world over as an architect who drafts modern buildings unlike anything seen before. Swirls and jitters of shining metal, swooping glass and unexpectedly curvy lines dominate Gehry's work, making architecture an experience rather than just a box.

383 PRETTY COOL THINGS

Well, we are at the point in the book that may make many readers angry. Some of you may believe that items in the following pages ought to have been in the Awesome section. To such readers as these I can only say that the delineation of what is Awesome and what is merely Cool was taken neither lightly nor soberly. My colleagues (the editors) and I have done our best to render what we felt were fair, if not always impartial, decisions. If you are still troubled by differences of opinion in these matters, try to remember that you may well have purchased this book in the impulse-buy section of your local marina or perhaps at the supermarket, next to a bin of remaindered milk, so, please, don't take any of it too seriously.

KEEPING WARM AND STYLISH

Balaclavas

Not to be confused with baklava, the tasty Mediterranean dessert, balaclavas are the woollen ski masks that used to be seen on school kids trudging home for lunch during the winter until the headwear was culturally hijacked by bank robbers who used them as disguises. Balaclavas have declined in popularity since the early 1980s, since they seem to label anyone who wears one as a potential criminal.

Hockey Jerseys

A sure sign that you're in Canada is passing people on the street wearing the jerseys of their favourite hockey team. Did Canadians start this tradition? Probably, since Canucks invented hockey as we know it (and no, I don't consider ancient European games that used a gnarled elderberry branch to smack a frozen ox turd around on a frozen puddle of ox urine to be "hockey as we know it"). During the 1970s, whenever rock band The Who passed through Toronto, singer Roger Daltrey would don a Maple Leafs jersey and, in a cool display of well-intentioned poor judgment, allowed himself to be photographed in it.

Tilley

After losing one too many hats overboard when sailing, Alex Tilley invented a floating hat, and so Tilley Endurables was founded. Now, the company has made its name with phenomenally expensive but phenomenally durable activewear that comes with various replacement guarantees. One ad featured a testimonial from a zookeeper who claimed that an elephant had eaten his Tilley hat and then later shat it out. After a good wash, the Tilley hat was as good as knew and perched back on its owner's head.

Lumber jackets

More correctly known as mackinaws (after the name of the red-and-black felt material they were once made of), these garments were indeed worn by hardy lumberjacks and other frontier types, but for many, their subliminal branding as "Canadian" occurred when they were coolly (and bafflingly) adopted as the default dress code of a certain subset of rock music–loving, unlaced-workboot-wearing suburban school kids from the 1970s to the 1980s.

Stanfield's

Based in Truro, Nova Scotia, Stanfield's is known as a manufacturer of underwear par excellence. (Have the words "underwear" and "par excellence" ever appeared in succession before? Could this be another cool Canadian first?) What is so cool about underwear? Well, two things. First, Stanfield's invented "unshrinkable" underwear to make sure men's junk would always have enough breathing room. Second, in 2010, they launched a massive campaign to raise money for testicular cancer research.

GOOD EATS

Dempster's Bread

For many Canadians, Dempster's bread is so universal that it comes as quite a surprise to learn that it is a "Canada only" brand (owned by Maple Leaf Foods). Dempster's is included here not only for its outstanding success as a Canadian brand but also for its malt bread—delicious, cylindrical loaves of dark bread that are seemingly not available west of Ontario but are no less cool for it.

The Pop Shoppe

Founded in London, Ontario, in 1969 and rising to prominence throughout the 1970s, the Pop Shoppe offered novel flavours of pop to consumers at reasonable prices and in clear, stubby bottles that echoed the (then) predominant style of beer bottles. By calling itself the "Pop Shoppe" and not the "Soda Shoppe," the firm immediately branded itself as a Canadian original. Despite rising and falling fortunes between the 1980s and the early 2000s, the Pop Shoppe has endured into the 21st century and continues to offer its cool flavour selection.

Maple Leaf Foods

Makers of meat, bread and who knows what else, Maple Leaf Foods does what Canadian business does best—it takes a national icon and makes it into a business logo. Whether it's the Hudson's Bay Company or BeaverTail pastry desserts, Canadian entrepreneurs seem to possess a cool genius for taking symbols of national character and converting them into retail opportunities. Canadians are not the only people to do this, but we do seem to be especially good at it.

Montréal Smoked Meat

This delicious species of cured beef is best experienced at one of Montréal's legendary delis, perhaps Schwartz's or Dunn's. Once, after ordering a smoked-meat platter at Schwartz's, I was amused to see that they had included some little "gherkins" around the edge of the plate as a token vegetable. Only when I bit into one did I realize that it was a tiny sausage, cleverly disguised as a gherkin. I shouldn't have been surprised—it was, after all, billed as a platter of meat, not a platter of meat and gherkins.

Redpath Sugar

Though now owned by American interests, Redpath Sugar still remains identified with its Canadian founders. The sweep of generations echoes behind the story of Redpath's humble roots in Québec in 1854. Cool but unsubstantiated rumours suggest that fermented waste from the firm's Toronto plant may have contributed for years to an entire generation of tipsy local wildlife.

Shreddies

This UK-based cereal brand is available in Canada and other Commonwealth countries. They are cool both for their marketing campaign to introduce new "diamond" Shreddies (that are regular old square Shreddies shown balanced on one corner), as well as for being the last cereal to offer a decent prize at the bottom of the box (alas, no more).

COOLLY DISTINCTIVE SNACKS

Dufflet's Bakery

Since 1975, Dufflet Rosenberg has been giving sweet-toothed Torontonians a reason to visit their dentists a little more often. With delicious but affordable cakes and treats available to order in Ontario and Québec, Dufflet has made a name for herself as central Canada's best worst-kept secret when it comes to quality cakes, pies and sweets.

Jos. Louis

Yes, these circular treats with a vanilla-paste core sandwiched between two layers of brown cake and covered in a thin layer of chocolate are uniquely Canadian. Invented by the mom and pop owners of Vachon bakeries and named after their two sons, Joseph and Louis, the name of a Jos. Louis, when spoken aloud is pronounced "Joe Loo-ee." This causes cool levels of confusion for visiting Americans who think you're mispronouncing the name of the late heavyweight boxing champion, Joe Lewis.

Ketchup- or Dill-flavoured Potato Chips

Whether these were invented in Canada is irrelevant; the cool part is that we're the only nation on earth that eats them. If Canada were to go into hiding for some sort of UN witness-protection program, all the bad guys would have to do to find us would be to figure out where the world's supply of ketchup or dill potato chips was going, and that's where we would be hiding.

Kraft Dinner

Invented by ex-pat Canuck J.L. Kraft, this entry's cool quotient comes from the fact that, although the same product is sold in the

U.S. as "Kraft Macaroni and Cheese," in Canada we appear to have insisted on our own culture-specific "Kraft Dinner," more often shortened to "KD." A reference to KD in the Barenaked Ladies song "If I had a Million Dollars" prompted fans to start throwing boxes of it at the stage during live shows. Tired of being pelted, the band requested that fans donate their boxes to local food banks.

Processed Cheese

It turns out that processed cheese (those sickly yellow slices of edible petroleum product so bland as to be barely distinguishable from the cellophane they are wrapped in and known as "American cheese") was also invented by J.L. Kraft, but admittedly only after he had moved to the U.S. and set up shop there. This entry is considered cool mainly because it gives us an opportunity to make fun of the tastes of Americans a bit, which, up until now, you've got to admit, we've been pretty restrained about.

COOL FOOD FOLKS

Susur Lee

Esteemed as an innovator in fusion cuisine (combining flavours from different parts of the world), Susur Lee's career has been built on the unexpected, with many of his establishments eschewing a set menu in favour of a "tasting" menu that sees Lee creating a daily menu inspired by fresh ingredients discovered at market. His career and international renown are as unconventional as his dishes are unexpected.

Christine Cushing (b. 1964)

A well-known TV chef and cookbook author, Cushing's career is a great Canadian success story. Her family emigrated from Greece when she was a one-year-old, and on her 34th birthday, while she was doing a product demonstration at the Canadian National Exhibition in Toronto, a TV producer in the crowd asked her if she'd wanted to audition for a new cooking show (which turned out to be *Dish It Out*). The rest, as they say, is history.

J.L. Kraft

The Canadian-born Kraft had much of his success after he moved to the U.S., but he is included here not for his eventual invention of Kraft Dinner, but rather because he made…cheese, and I, personally, think cheese is one of the coolest things that humanity has ever created. His invention of the abomination known as "processed cheese" notwithstanding, Kraft also made "real" cheese, rich in flavour and deliciously fatty. For making cheese, J.L. Kraft is, in this writer's opinion, worth of mention in any book of coolness.

Mr. Christie

"Mr. Christie, you make good cookies" is a marketing slogan known to almost all Canadians of a certain age. Breathlessly delivered by sticky-voiced children in a series of television commercials in the 1970s, it positioned the Mr. Christie brand as a familiar favourite with Canadian families. Eventually bought by Nabisco, itself owned by Kraft General Foods (see "J.L. Kraft," above), the Mr. Christie brand continues in Canada, a symbol of national identity strongly associated with kind-hearted, cookie-baking generosity.

McIntosh Apples

When American immigrant John McIntosh was clearing some land on his Ontario farm in the early 1800s, he discovered an apple tree whose fruit was sweeter than any he had ever tasted. Through grafting, McIntosh managed to create several more of these superior fruit-bearing trees, and so North America's most popular apple was born.

Stephen Yan

The irrepressible host of the CBC cooking show *Wok With Yan* seems to have dropped completely out of the public eye. Airing for two seasons in the early 1980s and with a handful of new shows in the early 1990s, each episode saw Yan leading viewers through a new recipe cooked in a wok. Every episode also featured Yan wearing an apron with a different wok-related pun of endearing awfulness: Wok Around the Clock; Danger: Men at Wok; Raiders of the Lost Wok; Wokkey Night in Canada and a succession of others too dreadful to contemplate. Stephen Yan, where are ye now?

THE NAKED TRUTH

Water-skiing squirrels. Scuba-diving cats. Glass-eating bearded ladies. None of these things are discussed in the following section, but they give you a good idea of the flavour (some might say "odour") of what follows. Here you will find an eclectic menagerie of eccentrics, dreamers and people who just like to take their clothes off. You will find uniquely built transit systems, improbably themed museums and stuffed toy animals thrown from hot air balloons. In short, here you will find Canada, in all of its warped glory.

Sons of Freedom

This "radical" sect of the communal-living, vegetarian and generally peace-nik Russian Doukhobor exiles staged nude demonstrations in the early 20th century to protest the Canadian government's policy toward group land ownership. As a point of interest, some Doukhobors also did their own plowing so as not to enslave their "brethren" animals.

Pothole Protest

In 2007, the residents of Leader, Saskatchewan, posed for a nude calendar to protest the dreadful state of the town's nearby highway. The road's potholes were so big that one model posed in his canoe, which fit in the pothole. One hopes that, for the sake of drivers and modest residents, the necessary road repairs were duly undertaken.

World Naked Bike Ride

This movement, if you can call it that, is not exclusive to Canada, but we appear to be enthusiastic participants. The annual ride, which is generally held in early June, is meant to draw attention to the dangers faced by cyclists and to raise awareness regarding oil dependency. Check your local listings to see if your community participates. Be sure to wear sunscreen. Sunglasses are allowed.

ONLY IN CANADA

Other uniquely Canadian things have already been included elsewhere in this book. The handful below are clumped together by virtue of being unexpected.

Trench Subways

Ontario is, apparently, one of the only places on earth to build subways by digging a trench and then filling it in again instead of tunnelling.

Metric System

The metric system has been officially adopted by every country on earth except Burma, Liberia and the U.S. But if you look at it from a (North) American point of view, the metric system is obviously something that only those whacky Canadians would get behind. That and milk in bags. Oh, and godless socialized medicine. Freaks.

Potato Museum

Yes, Canada has a museum dedicated to potatoes, located in, where else, Prince Edward Island. In case you didn't know, in addition to Anne of Green Gables and all that, PEI is also a world-famous (within Canada, anyway) grower of those apples of the earth known as potatoes. The museum boasts not only air conditioning but also a Potato Interpretive Centre. A giant fibreglass potato out front is more than four metres tall. Some days I can't believe I get paid to do this.

Purple Gas

In Canada, cheap fuel for agricultural use is dyed purple so that gas police can tell if farmers are using it for non-agricultural or personal use. Other countries use red, green yellow or blue dye, though a lot of countries use purple dye for aviation fuel.

Snowbirds

No, not retirees in Florida—every country has those. Rather, the acrobatic, fancy-flying team of the Canadian Forces.

Gopher Drop

To raise money for charity, the town of Cupar, Saskatchewan, holds this yearly event that sees a bagful of plush toy gophers dropped out of an air balloon. The gopher that lands closest to a hole in the ground "wins" first prize. Hell of a way to run a raffle.

Lloydminster

This Canadian city straddles the Alberta-Saskatchewan border and is officially a part of each province. Although Saskatchewan does not observe daylight savings time, Lloydminster does and adheres to Mountain Time as observed by Alberta. On the other hand, all the schools in the town follow the Saskatchewan educational curriculum. Confused yet? Each side of the city has postal codes that start with different letters, phone numbers with different area codes and wildly different insurance rates for drivers. Furthermore, each side of the city experiences different weather systems—okay, obviously I'm making that part up, but you get the idea.

COOL CLOCKS

Steam Clock

Built in 1977 by Canadian Raymond Saunders, Vancouver's steam clock in Gastown is a good deal newer than its Victorian sensibility would seem to suggest. Perhaps the most surprising thing about this clock is that it inevitably leads one to the discovery that, in this day and age, parts of downtown Vancouver are heated by a central steam system! It's only fair to point out that BC cities Port Coquitlam and Whistler also have examples of Saunders' steamy timekeepers.

Old Town Clock

In 1803, Edward, Duke of Kent for some reason decided that what Halifax really needed was…a clock. And not just any clock—a clock with a face on each of its four sides, visible from almost anywhere in town, thereby denying Haligonian laggards any possible excuse for being tardy. Had the town kept Edward waiting once somehow?

Clock Museum

If you're surrounded by youngsters who neither believe nor care that clocks once needed to be wound, you can overwhelm their skepticism or indifference with the evidence abundantly available at Canada's only clock museum in Deep River, Ontario. The soothing tick-tock of thousands of clocks is sure to send them into a semi-hypnotic state in which they will believe anything.

UNDUE POLITICAL PROCESS

I'm one of the few people who thinks that Canadian politics is excruciatingly dull (kidding, kidding—a lot of us do), but there are a handful of things that make politics a bit more interesting, even if only for a brief time. And here they are—all of them. This is it. There really aren't any more.

Bad Language

Whether it's a genuine burst of foul-mouthed rage or a ridiculously folksy-sounding euphemism, bad parliamentary language definitely livens things up. Some perennial favourites are "inspired by forty rod whiskey," "blatherskite," "dim-witted saboteur," "trained seal," "evil genius," "pompous ass" and Pierre Trudeau's immortal "fuddle duddle."

Crossing the Floor

This is a process by which a member of one party defects to another party, and it is often accompanied by great drama. For example, when Belinda Stronach crossed the floor from the Conservatives to the Liberals, it prevented the imminent fall of Paul Martin's government.

Filibustering

In effect, a filibuster occurs when a member (or members) of a political party, talk and talk and talk…and talk and talk and talk, in order to prevent (usually only postpone) a vote on a bill they oppose but are sure to lose. Rarely effective, filibustering is resorted to nowadays more as a metaphorically raised middle finger to the party with more votes.

Proroguing

A prime minister or premier can simply shut down Parliament, in effect, taking his or her ball and going home. A government usually resorts to proroguing Parliament when it knows it is sure to fall or simply can't be bothered to carry on doing its job.

INTREPID AND ADVENTUROUS

Simeon Perkins (1735–1812)

A staunch British loyalist and wealthy merchant, Simeon Perkins fielded numerous successful privateering expeditions during the American Revolutionary War, making a significant contribution to his already considerable fortune by sponsoring the capture and auction of U.S. ships.

Peter Pond (1739/40–1807)

This U.S. explorer and trader was implicated in two murders but retains an aura of cool for discovering the Alberta tar sands in 1778 when he noticed some Natives sealing their canoe with sticky, black goop. He thought nothing more of the goop aside from noting its usefulness in fixing canoes.

Bill Johnston (1782–1870)

This so-called "Pirate of the 1000 Islands" wanted Canada to join the U.S. and so set about stealing from vessels and house-holds in and around Kingston, Ontario. His most memorable exploit was first robbing and then torching the 45-metre-long steamship *Sir Robert Peel*. Along with his beautiful daughter Kate, Johnston led a life that reads more like a pulp-fiction melodrama than reality.

Sam Steele (1849–1919)

Sir Samuel Benfield Steele was the third officer inducted into the North West Mounted Police and had a notable and adventurous career. He participated in the last major battle between First Nations and Europeans to occur on Canadian soil, acting as a mainstay of government authority during the Klondike Gold Rush and later serving in the Boer War. Steele was a tough, no-nonsense frontier constable, with one of his typical diary entries reading, "Annual flogging administered to whores, adulterers, drunkards and gamblers."

Eddie Shack (b. 1937)

This likable but not particularly successful professional hockey player wore the jerseys of six different NHL teams between 1959 and his retirement in 1975. Although he scored a Stanley Cup–winning goal for the Toronto Maple Leafs in 1963, Shack always claimed that the puck had bounced off his rear end and into the net as he was trying to get out of the way. Popular as an "agitator," Shack spawned a hit novelty song in 1966 called "Clear the Track, Here Comes the Shack." After he retired, he became a spokesman for soft-drink retailer The Pop Shoppe and embarked on a series of happy adventures to capitalize on his name, such as shaving off his luxuriant moustache for Schick razors and selling Christmas trees out of suburban parking lots.

Jaymz Bee (b. 1963)

Based in Toronto but wreaking his happy chaos of parties, jazz music and good times all across this great land, Jaymz Bee launched his admirably eclectic career as a founding member of the Al Waxman Fan Club, which involved writing songs that celebrated the titular actor (1935–2001) and his starring role in the *King of Kensington* TV series (1975–80). Bee then fronted a succession of bands such as The Bee People, Look People and, later, Jaymz Bee and His Royal Jelly Orchestra. Bon vivant extraordinaire, Bee has toured Europe, the U.S. and Canada with his heart-on-the-sleeve brand of sincere fabulousness, sharp suits and cocktails.

COOL WARRIORS

James Wolfe (1727–59)

Along with Louis Joseph de Montcalm (see below), the memory of Wolfe will forever be associated with the Battle of the Plains of Abraham (1759), when Wolfe's forces defeated Montcalm's, sounding the death knell for French rule in Canada. Most of Wolfe's coolness comes from his audacity in plotting an attack that was so risky and so full of holes that it really ought not to have worked, but it did.

Louis Joseph de Montcalm (1712–59)

As James Wolfe's opposite number during the Battle of the Plains of Abraham, Montcalm really only makes it into the cool category by dint of his association with this famous battle. In reality, he was a staggeringly complacent general who didn't think the British would attack such a difficult position, had given most of the militia time off to go help with the harvest and had numerous opportunities beforehand to rout the English forces, but followed through on none of them.

Isaac Brock (1769–1812)

This British general is one of the best-remembered soldiers of the War of 1812. He was smart, decisive and had keen insight into what his opponents might be thinking or planning. By many accounts, Tecumseh (see below), after meeting him, is alleged to have said, "This is a man!"

Tecumseth (1768–1813)

This Shawnee warrior and leader was a key player in the War of 1812. He used his leadership skills to forge an alliance of First Nations to fight alongside the British against the Americans. Although the British ultimately betrayed the First Nations following the death of both Tecumseh and Isaac Brock, Tecumseh's personal example of strength, courage and integrity has inspired people ever since.

Roy Brown (1893–1944)

For many years, Roy Brown (of Carlton Place, Ontario) was officially credited with shooting down the infamous Red Baron (Manfred von Richthofen) during World War I. More recent scholarship strongly suggests that it was a bullet from Australian ground gunners that ended Richthofen's life. Still, anyone who tangles with the Red Baron and not only lives, but also gets in a few good shots, is clearly cool in our books.

Billy Bishop (1894–1956)

With 72 confirmed kills to his credit, Billy Bishop (of Owen Sound, Ontario) is well known as Canada's pre-eminent World War I flying ace.

Wilfrid "Wop" May (1896–1952)

One of Canada's early aviation heroes, May was being chased by Manfred von Richthofen during the dogfight that ended the infamous Red Baron's reign. After the war, May became a heroic bush pilot, helping to fly desperately needed medicine to the far north and participating in the hunt for the so-called Mad Trapper, Albert Johnson. He led a truly cool (and at times freezing) life of adventure.

Arthur Currie (1875–1933)

Although he had served in the militia for years, Currie had no professional military experience when he was appointed commander of the newly formed Canadian Corps during World War I. But he soon proved himself to be a masterful planner, helping to oversee preparations for the Battle of Vimy Ridge. He later became principal and vice-chancellor of McGill University despite having no post-secondary education.

The Dalton Boys

Charles Dalton (1910–98) and his younger brother Elliott (d. 1994) are emblematic of the common fighting man. They were both wounded leading men ashore during the D-Day offensive in 1944, but they quickly recovered and returned to active service until the end of the war. They were both awarded the Distinguished Service Order.

Roméo Dallaire (b. 1946)

As the leader of the UN Peacekeeping force in Rwanda in the early 1990s, Dallaire asked for but was denied permission to take military action to prevent the Rwandan genocide of 1994, during which 800,000 people were murdered. He has since become an advocate for people affected by war, particularly children.

COOLLY TOLERANT

Amish

This Mennonite subsect is famous for dressing plainly and eschewing many forms of modern technology, most notably the automobile. In and around Ontario's Kitchener-Waterloo region, Amish farmers can often be seen driving horse-and-buggy rigs. Amish folk also make delicious maple syrup, cookies and sausages.

Sharon Temple

In 1801, David Willson, the leader of a religious group called the Children of Peace, settled in the little community of Sharon, Ontario. Between 1821 and 1825, he hired renowned builder Ebeneezer Dean to construct a series of beautiful wooden buildings that have survived to the present day. The structures are well cared for and still as remarkable as when they were first built.

BLASTS FROM THE PAST

Travelling back in time is definitely cool. Consider each of the following entries to be a portal into the past. In some cases, you may have to pay the price of admission, but that should in no way diminish your appreciation of the awesomosity coolness that awaits you. If your favourite or local site seems to be missing, don't worry; it's probably in a different section of this book.

Barkerville
At this fully restored 19th-century gold-mining town in BC, visitors can pan for gold, tour the buildings and shops and cap off the day with an authentic old-time vaudeville(-esque) show.

Black Creek Pioneer Village

This outdoor museum is a pleasing mish-mash of 19th-century buildings all moved to the site in Ontario during the 20th century. The emphasis is on the 1860s, with a working tinsmith's shop, a general store and a Mennonite meeting house.

Village Historique Acadien
A vanished way of life is depicted in this 364-hectare Acadian village in New Brunswick that includes functioning farms, a smithy for metal-working, a bakery and a tavern.

Lunenberg

Famous as the home of the *Bluenose II* replica schooner, Lunenberg, Nova Scotia, is also a UNESCO World Heritage Site, since it is an almost perfectly preserved example of a planned British colonial settlement.

Sherbrooke Village

Credited as the "largest living history museum" in the province, Sherbrooke Village, Nova Scotia, truly is a town frozen in time (well, more accurately, "restored" back in time) where visitors can have their photos taken on glass plates.

ECHOES PAST AND PRESENT

Gopher Hole Museum

For anyone (farmers) who has ever been driven crazy by gophers, Torrington, Alberta's Gopher Hole Museum offers an attraction that is equal parts morbid and cute—taxidermied gophers dressed up like humans and posed in little dioramas of eclectic human activities: driving miniature chuckwagons, hunting miniature wildfowl and clubbing tiny lizards to death.

Just Enough Unexploded Ordnance to Make it Interesting

Somewhere back in the days of World War II, someone hit on the idea of using live ordnance for target practice when training Canadian soldiers to go overseas and fight. Decades passed, and the formerly desolate areas used for target practice became populated with bedroom communities with unexploded shells in their parks and playgrounds. Watch where you step!

Caddy Lake Rock Tunnels

In 1877, the intrepid builders of the Canadian Pacific Railway blasted tunnels through the rock surrounding Caddy Lake in what is now Manitoba's Whiteshell Provincial Park (130 kilometres east of Winnipeg). Now you can canoe through the tunnels and reach out to touch the past even as you seek a bit of shade on a hot day.

Underground City

Beneath the streets of Montréal is the famous Underground City, which contains more than 30 kilometres of subterranean consumer bliss, including 1600 shops and 200 other establishments such as restaurants, movie theatres and hotels.

Sugar Shacks

Wherever you find syrup-producing maple forests, you will find sugar shacks. Resembling small houses, these structures are a cool artifact of making delicious maple syrup.

SS Klondike Historic Site

Although it is no longer functional, the rebuilt steam-powered paddle steamer *Klondike* (originally built in 1921) is a National Historic Site in Yukon. It is known for its storied past, which includes sinking once and being rebuilt to sail (or steam) again.

Sainte-Marie Among the Hurons

In 1639, a mixed settlement of Jesuits and Hurons was founded near present-day Midland, Ontario. Declared a national historic site in 1920, a re-creation of this European–First Nations settlement has since been built there. Moments of quiet amid the tour groups can create a profound sense of connection to Canada's often contradictory past of cultures clashing, mixing and clashing again.

FUNNY MONEY

We Can Make the Queen Smile Inappropriately

Take a $20 bill (bearing the Queen's likeness) and make a sharp vertical fold down the centre of the Queen's face and again down the centre of each eye. You'll now have a bill with three sharp creases in it. Tilt the bill toward or away from you to see the Queen adopt either a vapid smile or a hangdog grimace. You're welcome.

We Can Make Wilfrid Laurier Look Like Mr. Spock

No matter which version of the $5 bill you have, by drawing some pointy ears, arched eyebrows and a black bowl haircut on Wilfrid Laurier's visage, you can make him look like Mr. Spock. You might think that doodling these features on anyone would make that person look like Mr. Spock, but Laurier's lips, philtrum and bone structure do have a highly (Leonard) Nimoyan sense about them.

COOL STRUCTURES

CN Tower

At 553 metres tall, the CN Tower (completed in 1976) is the most easily recognized landmark on the Toronto skyline. And during a thunderstorm, you might get to see one of its 72 yearly lightning strikes!

Bata Shoe Museum

As if a collection of more than 12,000 shoes isn't cool enough (if you go in for that sort of thing), this museum in Toronto is supposed to look like a gigantic shoebox, though I personally think it looks more like a massive shoe, but what do I know?

Robarts Library

From a certain perspective, the U of T's central library resembles a giant concrete turkey, shaped perhaps by the brutalist school of modern architecture.

Inuvik Church and Town Hall

Although its dome wouldn't be out of place in a Romanesque church, the patterns on the building's exterior walls make it look like a big igloo!

Calgary Tower

With a rotating restaurant on the observation level, the Calgary Tower (completed in 1968) is 180.5 metres tall and a great place to see the city sights (from afar) or have a lovely meal.

Skylon Tower

Completed in 1965, this 160-metre observation tower in Niagara Falls is somehow much more futuristic-looking than the CN Tower in spite of being 11 years older.

BRIDGING THE GAP

Capilano Suspension Bridge

I have only seen or done a handful of the many awesome and cool things mentioned in this book, but happily crossing the Capilano Suspension Bridge is one of them. And let me tell you, wading into space along this slender bridge suspended 20 metres over the lush valley of BC's Capilano River is a moving and invigorating experience.

First and Second Narrows Bridges

Both remarkable feats of construction, the Lion's Gate (First Narrows) and Ironworkers' Memorial (Second Narrows) bridges connect Vancouver to the North Shore. They give the city a unique and amazing character, especially during rush hour.

Confederation Bridge

Called "one of Canada's top engineering achievements of the 20th century," the nearly 13-kilometre-long Confederation Bridge connects Prince Edward Island to New Brunswick. That's one big bridge—the world's longest over icy waters, apparently.

JUST FOR FUN

Whoopee Cushion

It appears to be true—the Canadian firm JEM Rubber was the first to create and market an inflatable rubber bladder for the purpose of making a fart sound. In the early 1930s, a rival U.S. company took the idea and ran with it (JEM having failed to secure a patent), and so flatulent prank history was made.

Billy Jamieson

A combination of P.T. Barnum and Indiana Jones, Billy Jamieson (1954–2011) was Canada's foremost collector and curator of shrunken heads, sacred amulets and blowpipes. He bought out the curious contents of the Niagara Falls Museum, including an Egyptian mummy that later proved to be that of the pharaoh Ramses I.

The Sour Toe Cocktail Club

At the Downtown Hotel in Dawson City, Yukon, you can become a member of this club by drinking any alcoholic beverage that contains a dehydrated human big toe (kept on the premises). The toe must touch your lips, but no swallowing is allowed. The custom started with the amputation of a rum-runner's toe in the 1920s. Upon the toe's discovery 50 years later, the tradition of the Sour Toe cocktail began. All was well until 1980, when someone accidentally swallowed the toe. The club is now on toe number eight, the interim toes having been given by willing donors who lost their big toes for one reason or another (usually it's "another").

SHOP UNTIL YOU DROP

The Distillery District

The former Gooderham and Worts Distillery in Toronto is now the largest intact collection of Victorian industrial buildings in North America. Happily, developers have filled all the excellent brown brick buildings with shops, cafés and art galleries.

Gastown

Named after a talkative 1870s saloon owner nicknamed "Gassy Jack," Vancouver's Gastown was once the centre of the city's drinking scene, but the area had fallen into decay by the 1960s. After it was declared a national historic site in the early 1970s, Gastown's many heritage buildings were developed into stores, restaurants and other businesses.

Old Montréal

Anywhere else, horse-drawn carriage tours would just seem cheesy, but amid the winding cobblestone streets and old stone buildings, the clip-clop of horse's hooves helps to complete the impression that you are travelling centuries back in time.

Eastern Townships

These quiet little communities in southeastern Québec are populated by cottagers and hobby farmers with a healthy winter ski industry thrown in for good measure. They're a cool place to summer with a stack of mystery novels and some sandals.

Kensington Market

Eclectic. Bohemian. Eccentric. No matter how you describe it, this little patchwork of streets, houses and businesses in Toronto is a unique quilt of second-hand clothing shops, art stores, cafés and bars, interspersed with greengrocers, butchers and cheese shops, all gloriously and resolutely untainted by the upscale trendiness that has destroyed much of Toronto's character in other neighbourhoods.

ByWard Market

Ottawa used to be called Bytown, after British military engineer John By. ByWard Market is a sprawling but orderly warren of indoor and outdoor shops, souvenir stands, snack bars and restaurants where it's possible to become pleasantly lost.

Yorkville

In the 1960s and '70s, this little chunk of real estate in the heart of Toronto boasted a bustling underground scene of hippies, coffee houses and other less-savoury pursuits. But somehow, as the 1970s progressed, Yorkville morphed into an enclave of chic clothing stores, art galleries, tobacconists, purveyors of fancy writing implements, restaurants and bars. Nowadays, there's nary a hippy to be found, but you can buy a $1600 blouse if you want.

Mahone Bay

This little Nova Scotia town's motto tells you everything you need to know: "A Treasure Since 1754." Generally regarded as one of the most picturesque towns on the East Coast, its three famous churches (Anglican, Lutheran and United) give it the air of a post-card come to life.

COOL STRETCHES OF STREETS

Commercial Drive

Also known as "The Drive," this Vancouver street is noted for its "safe alternative" vibe, with many vegetarian and health-food restaurants and highly diverse ethnography. Anyone wanting to see a little slice of "Vangroovy" is advised not to miss it.

Robson Street

Those visiting Vancouver and hoping for a more upscale experience should take a cruise along Robson Street, with its chic shops and many fine dining establishments. If you're there on a summer weekend, you may get to see an informal parade of classic cars cruising the strip.

Tunnels of Moose Jaw

In the 1920s, up and down Moose Jaw's historic Main Street, bootleggers and Chinese immigrants may (or may not) have used tunnels and passageways between basements of buildings for rum-running or illegal gambling. You can decide for yourself by visiting the Tunnels of Moose Jaw exhibit and tour, which paints a vibrant picture of a different time in the life of this Saskatchewan city.

Portage and Main

Famously mispronounced by people who don't know any better, Winnipeg's Portage (pronounced like "porridge") and Main is hailed as Canada's windiest intersection. Whether it is or isn't is irrelevant because this undoubtedly blustery crossroads is firmly established as one of the many cool things to venerate in the True North Strong and Free (and windy).

Yonge Street

Its status as "the world's longest street," is utterly dubious, but it is, arguably, Canada's most famous. Although the good-hearted aura of jolly sleaze that defined Yonge Street, Toronto, in the 1970s has been largely supplanted by far less questionable businesses, if you walk south from Bloor Street, there is still enough naughtiness for an enjoyable stroll while you sip your Starbucks and look for a good place to buy Mountie souvenirs.

Queen West

What was once Toronto's must-see bohemian enclave of whole-sale fabric stores, beaderies, used-book shops, boutique restaurants, music clubs and overpriced clothes has now morphed into a chic, upscale mixture of wholesale fabric stores, beaderies, boutique restaurants, music clubs and overpriced clothes—the used-book trade is the only thing that has really suffered.

Rue Sherbrooke

Montréal's rue Sherbrooke simply oozes wealth and...well, wealth. Expensive shops and opulent churches service the corporeal and spiritual needs of moneyed Montréalers. Holt Renfrew got its start here—that alone should tell you as much as you need to know.

Rue St. Catherine

Known to every Montréaler and famous all across the country, rue St. Catherine is a major thoroughfare that includes concert venue Place des Arts, much of Montréal's gay village and great shopping (as well as, formerly, a high concentration of strip clubs, now greatly reduced in number).

CHURCHES IN QUÉBEC

All of Québec's magnificent churches truly make la belle province seem like Canada's own little corner of Europe (well, that and all the other old—for Canada—buildings and structures). I submit for your consideration, four of the largest, most impressive and most famous—in short, a divine quartet of cool.

Basilique Notre-Dame de Montréal

With various features dating from the mid-to-late 19th century, Montréal's basilica boasts monolithic Classical-Gothic architecture, radiant stained-glass windows, a pipe organ and some of the most ornate and opulent wood carving to be found on this side of the Atlantic. And remember, it was built entirely by hand.

Basilique Notre-Dame de Québec

A national historic site, the plot of land on which the basilica sits has been the site of four separate buildings since 1647, three of which were destroyed by fire, with the fourth being torn down by the British in 1759 (how Canadian). The present, and very impressive structure dates from the 1920s.

Basilica of Sainte-Anne-de-Beaupré

Before its construction in 1922, this massive basilica was preceded by no less than four other churches on the site, the first being a small chapel built after a 1650 coming-ashore by a group of grateful sailors who had survived a shipwreck. Saint Anne is the patron saint of Québec.

Séminaire de Québec

Built in the 17th century and steadily added to over the next 200 years, the seminary takes visitors on a warm, beautiful and majestic tour of 300 years worth of sprawling religious architecture.

PARKS

You're going to have to take my word for it that all of the following places are pretty cool, since to do more than hint at the true depth, breadth and sheer magnitude of their coolness would rapidly gobble up all the remaining space of this book. If you don't believe me, go see for yourself.

Nahanni National Park Reserve

Three massive river canyons in this Northwest Territories park make for great whitewater rafting, and the Virginia Falls are twice as high as Niagara Falls. Don't get us started on the sheer variety of wildlife.

Glacier National Park

This park in BC has amazing hiking trails and more than 400 glaciers, but watch out for avalanches.

Muncho Lake Provincial Park

Also in BC, this park has amazingly varied terrain, mountains, lakes, wildlife and a much vaunted…bog!

Pacific Rim National Park

Kayaking and scuba diving amid the Broken Group Islands, walking along great trails, surfing at Long Beach and watching whales pretty much sums it up for this BC park.

Yoho National Park

Two beautiful mountain lakes (Emerald and O'Hara), Takakkaw Falls, the Kicking Horse River, a natural stone bridge imaginatively called "Natural Bridge" and Hoodoo Creek, populated with the top-heavy stone towers known as hoodoos, all make this park in BC a must-see.

Athabasca Sand Dunes Provincial Park

Sand dunes. Big ones. The most northerly sand dune area in the world. This park in Alberta is only accessible by plane so you'd better be a total sand dune geek if you're planning to go.

Fish Creek Provincial Park

Smack dab in south Calgary, Fish Creek is recognized as one of world's largest urban parks, offering a pleasing slice of wilderness amid the wilds of the city.

Jasper National Park

You can ride the Jasper Tramway cable car, canoe on Pyramid Lake, hike Maligne Canyon, enjoy a soak in Miette Hot Springs, savour the sights of Medicine Lake, climb parts of Mount Edith Cavell or observe the 400-year-old Columbia Icefield in this Alberta park.

Waterton Lakes National Park

This park in southern Alberta has spectacular mountains and lakes, a shared ecosystem with U.S. Glacier National Park and an unusual geological feature somewhat suggestively named the "Lewis Overthrust."

Cypress Hills Interprovincial Park

Straddling Alberta and Saskatchewan (trust me, it's not a comfort-able position), this is Canada's only park dedicated to gangsta rap, namely the U.S. hip-hop group Cypress Hill. Kidding, kidding. Really, though, you can see trumpeter swans and chickadees, as well as the site of the famous Cypress Hill Massacre in 1873.

Fundy National Park

See the world's highest tides in this New Brunswick park inundate the land and then walk out on squishy sands for nearly a kilometre when the tides go out.

Kouchibouguac National Park

This coolly named park in New Brunswick has a mixed maritime environment that includes a windswept sand dune beach, salt marshes and forests. You can also take a canoe tour to visit a grey seal colony.

Prince Edward Island National Park

Personally, I'd go to see the stretch of red sandstone cliffs that drop dramatically into the Atlantic Ocean, but the biggest attraction is probably Green Gables house, which inspired Lucy Maud Montgomery to write *Anne of Green Gables*. Just think if the original owners had chosen a different colour, it could have been *Anne of Red Windows.*

Kejimkujik National Park

Pristine beaches, magnificent forests, camping, canoeing and… stargazing. This park in Nova Scotia is an officially designated "Dark Sky Reserve" under the aegis of the Royal Astronomical Society of Canada.

Terra Nova National Park

Flora, fauna, fjords and—leaping to the other end of the alphabet—whale watching are all part of the beauty of this park in Newfoundland and Labrador.

Gros Morne National Park

This park in Newfoundland and Labrador is a UN World Heritage Site, and you can step on to the earth's mantle where it pushes through the terrestrial crust.

MINIATURE DESERTS

We now move from the oversized to the small. We normally think of deserts as vast, howling expanses of blowing sand, but as the next few entries show, they can also be small—cool little pockets of sandy terrain in unexpected places.

Pingos

The Tuktoyuktuk Peninsula in the Northwest Territories itself is not a desert, but it does contain approximately 1400 "pingos," which are piles of sand that may be anywhere from 15 metres to half a kilometre across. Pingos are shaped like volcanoes, often with water in the "crater."

Pocket Desert

Located in pleasingly named Osoyoos at the southern end of the Okanagan Valley in BC, the Pocket Desert is such a delicate eco-system that a boardwalk has been constructed so that visitors can view the desert without harming it.

Great Sand Hills

What's so great about these hills in southwestern Saskatchewan you ask? I would posit that encountering 1900 square kilometres of sand dunes and flats is undoubtedly cool. We should point out that the province is also home to another little desert—see the entry for the Athabasca Sand Dunes (p. 249).

Spirit Sands Dune Field

Sitting like an out-of-place postage stamp, these 4 square kilometres of dunes in Manitoba up to 30 metres tall (!) are a surprising discovery that awaits you at Spruce Woods Provincial Park.

SEEDS OF PLENTY

Grain

It's almost become a tired stereotype to say that Canada has grown so much grain that we've been called the World's Breadbasket, but this doesn't stop it from being true. For two of our Grainest Hits, you need look no further than names like Red Fife and Marquis.

Ginseng

Valued as a prolonger of life in traditional Asian medicines, since the 1980s, ginseng has become eastern Canada's "little crop that could."

Canola

First bred in Manitoba, grown on the Prairies and processed in eastern Canada, this strain of rapeseed and the oil extracted from it are Canadian inventions designed to reduce the presence of harmful fatty acids present in other cooking oils.

Semex

Everyone knows that Canada is a world-class purveyor of grain, lumber and petroleum products, but bull semen? Since 1959, the Canadian company Semex (head office in Guelph, Ontario) has been one of the world's leaders in selling bull semen, embryos and other "must-have" genetic material for serious breeders of cattle.

Beef

Once you've inseminated your shiny new embryo (see "Semex," above), you can grow it into a delicious cow. As a big fan of meat, I'm excited to see my country excel at producing a product that is close to (if not good for) my heart.

WATER DWELLERS

Eels

It's surprising to me that Canada even has eels, and that's why they're included as cool creatures (yes, it's subjective). Besides being typically wiggly, as eels are prone to be, they can live up to 25 years, and North American eels complete an epic round-trip journey of between 2000 and 6000 kilometres—they are born in the Atlantic Ocean, swim to rivers to mature, and then return to the ocean to spawn.

Giant Squid

Atlantic Canada is (or once was) home to the largest confirmed giant squid. In 1878, fishermen discovered the still-living beast near Thimble Tickle Cove in Newfoundland. Its body was 7 metres long, and it had 11-metre tentacles with suckers 40 centimetres wide! It was promptly chopped up into dog food.

Sturgeon

Sturgeon are amazing fish—they can live for well over 100 years, and some freshwater varieties can reach nearly 4 metres long and weigh more than 500 kilograms. BC's Frasier River is notable for catches of several specimens of this size. We are pleased to say that they are tagged and released back into the wild.

Trout

In 2007, twin brothers Adam and Sean Konrad were fishing in Saskatchewan's Lake Diefenbaker when they landed one of the largest rainbow trout on record, measuring nearly a metre from mouth to tail, almost as big around and weighing almost 20 kilograms.

BUSINESS AS USUAL

North West Company

From 1779 to 1821, the North West Company (NWC) gave the Hudson's Bay Company (HBC) a run for their money, successfully outmanoeuvring their competitors by being more aggressive and creative in their tactics and strategies. Although what was supposed to be an 1821 merger between the two turned into the absorption of the NWC by the HBC, the machinations of the NWC profoundly shaped Canada's history.

Lee Valley

This company started out in the early 1980s as a mail-order service for fine woodworking tools. It has since flourished, with select retail locations and a reputation for innovative, high-quality products as practical as they are unexpected (for example, giant slippers to don over muddy boots when tracking in and out of a house) in a wide range of areas, but the company still focuses on woodworking and gardening.

Overwaitea

Included for its hilarious name, this BC grocery chain started out as a general store that generously added a couple of ounces to every pound of tea.

Shaw

A monolith of TV, cable and Internet services, this company is still presided over by the Canadian family whose name it bears.

FAMILY AFFAIRS

Hills

Since the turn of the 20th century, the Hills have been Regina's most prominent family, starting out in real estate development but swiftly moving into oil and gas, insurance and broadcasting.

Stronachs

Frank Stronach (b. 1932) is the founder of Magna International, a manufacturer of auto parts. His daughter, Belinda Stronach (b. 1966), was both a Conservative and a Liberal politician, scandalously crossing the floor in 2005, thereby saving Paul Martin's Liberal government from falling. After her brief flirtation with politics, she returned to high-profile posts at Magna.

Westons

When George Weston (1864–1924) founded his eponymous bakery in 1882, it was the start of a family empire. The family today owns Loblaws as well as the UK department store Selfridge's. Galen Weston Sr. is routinely mentioned as one of the wealthiest men in Canada. His wife, Hilary, was the 26th lieutenant-governor of Ontario, while their son, Galen Jr., is moving into various aspects of the family business.

OUT IN THE WILD

Canoeing

Considering the canoe's storied past in Canada's history, you'd think that someone would have named this activity as Canada's official mode of non-motorized transportation by now, but no one has.

Chilkoot Trail

Initially a First Nations trading route, this 53-kilometre pathway straddles the Alaska-BC border. Prospectors and outfitters during the Klondike Gold Rush eventually took over the trail. This comparatively remote location boasted an "aerial tramway" (cable car) to hoist supplies over the heads of prospectors. Today it is used for hiking and sightseeing.

Hiking

When you're the second largest country in the world, needless to say, you've got a bit of space. What better way to "fill" it than with hiking trails so that everyone can enjoy it.

Kayaking

Not just for the Arctic any more, kayaks have made their way to lakes, rivers and shorelines all across Canada.

Sailing

Canada's lakes, rivers and coasts offer some of the best sailing in North America and, indeed, the world.

Scuba Diving

It's not just that we have great scuba diving (which we do), but whether it's coastal artificial reefs, flooded ghost towns or sunken ships, Canada also has some of the most *interesting* scuba diving going.

Snowboarding

We have hills. We have snow. We have boards. You do the math.

Tobogganing

Mellow and/or exhilarating (sometimes all at the same time), sliding down a snow-covered hill on a small sled has filled happy winter days in this country for generations.

TransCanada Trail

Though still in process at the time of writing this book, once completed, the trail will be the largest recreational trail network in the world at 23,000 kilometres. Begun in 1992 for Canada's 125th birthday, it has pavilions at various points along the trail where donors can have their name, or a loved one's, inscribed for the ages.

West Coast Trail

This 75-kilometre trail along the southwestern portion of Vancouver Island offers some of the most beautiful scenery anywhere in Canada.

THE EYE OF THE BEHOLDER

A House Built From…

In my opinion, something qualifies as art if it elicits an emotional response, be it amazement, disgust or bafflement. While the topics in this section can be considered profound reflections of a certain culture or socio-economic lifestyle, this story is just plain weird—an eccentric one-off, as it were. Starting in 1952, retired mortician David Brown began building moderately a palatial house from…empty embalming fluid bottles. You can decide for yourself whether it qualifies as art. It stands today at 11341 Highway 3A, about 40 kilometres north of Creston, BC.

Rue du Trésor

Really a tiny, closed-off alley in Québec City, Rue du Trésor is a happy stumble-upon for unsuspecting visitors who may want to immortalize their trip by having a caricature done of themselves. Or perhaps you're looking for affordable prints and sketches showing scenes from French Canadian life. Or maybe you just enjoy discovering unexpected enclaves—secret nooks of culture tucked away from the hurly-burly of modern life.

Rue des Artistes

Though also renowned as something of a tourist trap, Montréal's Rue des Artistes is a wonderful way to peruse the offerings of both artists and art dealers. Really, pretty much anything you do in Montréal is going to be cool, but since this is the art section of this book, I couldn't leave this one out.

Cornelius Krieghoff (1815–72)

When you have a name like Cornelius Krieghoff, you're sort of cool by default, but when you're also one of the first artists to take an interest in distinctly Canadian scenes, your coolness quotient goes up quite a bit. Krieghoff enjoyed rustic winter scenes often showing cozy-looking buildings and labourers, as well as teams of horses against snowy backgrounds that come across as far more inviting than they probably were.

Homer Watson (1855–1936)

Honoured by a curator at the National Gallery of Canada as "the man who first saw Canada as Canada, rather than as dreamy blurred pastiches of European painting," this noted landscape painter was also called "Canada's Constable" (a famous British landscapist) by none other than Oscar Wilde. When you consider that Homer also attended séances with William Lyon Mackenzie King, he is clearly one of Canada's cool people.

Loring and Wyle

Between them, this dynamic duo of early to mid-20th-century Canadian sculptors designed and created many World War I monuments as well as busts and statues of prominent political figures of the day. Though both American-born, Florence Wyle

(1881–1968) and Frances Loring (1887–1982) settled in Toronto. In addition to their prolific output as sculptors, their working relationship spawned the burning question that, even now, no one has answered: Were the two women lovers? It makes no difference to their renowned work, but as Canadians, we're interested in the life stories of interesting people, so we want to know!

Doris McCarthy (1910–2010)

Besides living for 100 years, Doris McCarthy was a prolific painter who travelled widely in an age well before arts council grants. Honoured and fêted throughout her long and productive career, she taught, thought, wrote and inspired others by the example she set, as well as by her staggering output of canvases. I take pride in noting that, for a time, she lived in my grandparents' basement in Toronto's Beaches neighbourhood.

Great Public TV

With most provinces having their own unique public television station (usually incorporating the name of the province; for example, TV Ontario, CTV Two Alberta), documentaries, public affairs and kids' programming are in good hands—though almost always embattled because of funding difficulties.

City TV Model

After it started in Toronto, City TV's model of hyper-local reporting, mobile reporters with a single camera and a microphone, as well as an "open" studio where production and support staff were visible working in the background, spread to cities all across Canada.

Dreadful Sitcoms

In the 1970s and '80s, Canada produced TV sitcoms so awful that they now enjoy a sort of retro cool. I'm speaking of such timeless anti-classics as *Trouble with Tracy, Hangin In, Snow Job* and a select handful of others too dreadful to name.

Great Sitcoms

Happily, with the turn of the new millennium, Canadian TV producers seemed to find their stride and started making good shows such as *Corner Gas* and *Little Mosque on the Prairie* (both now concluded).

COOL ENTERTAINERS

Faye Wray (1907–2004)

Wray screamed her way to fame playing Ann Darrow, King Kong's love interest in the original 1933 film. She is widely considered to be the first "scream queen."

Jay Silverheels (1912–80)

This Mohawk actor was famous for playing Tonto opposite Clayton Moore as the Lone Ranger on television from 1949 to 1957 and in subsequent media appearances.

Bruno Gerussi (1928–95)

This actor was famous for playing the character of Nick Adonidas in the long-running CBC TV show, *The Beachcombers*.

Rich Little (b. 1938)

Nicknamed "The Man of a Thousand Voices," Little has built a career on the voices of others, honing his impressions of politicians and celebrities to the point that if you're not looking at him, it may be impossible to tell whether you're listening to Rich Little or the individual he's impersonating.

Eugene Levy (b. 1946)

While he is famous for mainstream Hollywood successes such as the *American Pie* series, most Canadians fondly remember this comedian for his endless series of characters on *SCTV*, many of which happily required him to cross his eyes.

Lorne Cardinal (b. 1964)

This Cree actor from Alberta is probably best known as Quinton Davis on the TV sitcom *Corner Gas*.

Pam Anderson (b. 1967)

Famous for her role on the TV show *Baywatch* (original series 1989–1999), this blonde, bust-enhanced actress and model also holds the record for appearing the most times on the cover of *Playboy* magazine.

Adam Beach (b. 1972)

Of Salteaux heritage, Beach has appeared in numerous roles on both sides of the border.

Grace Park (b. 1974)

An actress in the teen soap *Edgemont*, Park has also starred in the remake of *Battlestar Galactica* and in *Hawaii Five-O*.

Tricia Helfer (b. 1974)

Model, actress and famous as the host of *Canada's Next Top Model*, she also played Cylon Number Six in the TV remake of *Battlestar Galactica*.

Stana Katic (b. 1978)

This actress is best known for appearing alongside fellow Canuck Nathan Fillion on the mystery series *Castle*.

Ellen Page (b. 1987)

Noted for playing the title role in *Juno*, Page has also appeared in other high-profile and well-received films.

COOL ARTS AND MEDIA

CHANNEL SURFING

(The) Beachcombers (CBC)

This perennial dramedy's central characters lived in a small West Coast town, where they salvaged logs that had broken from logging booms. If you were one of the millions of Canadians who *didn't* watch it, this show seemed to run *forever,* always taking up a prime spot in the TV line-up where you'd been hoping to see something a bit more interesting (I speak from experience). It ran for so long that they finally dropped the "The" in the title, in the hope that "Beachcombers" would sound more contemporary—it didn't, and the show finally hung up its gloves in 1990 after *18 years* on the air.

Cash Cab (various networks)

It's not really Canadian, but rather the Canuck version of a much-franchised idea (such as *Pop/American/Canadian Idol*), but we still like the idea of randomly jumping into a cab and getting to answer questions for money.

Cold Squad (CTV)

This procedural crime drama followed investigators who tried to crack unsolved crimes from years earlier. It ran from 1997 to 2005 and starred the lovely Julie Stewart.

DaVinci's Inquest (CBC)

This drama, starring Nicholas Campbell, was based on the improbable election of a former coroner to the mayoralty. Amazingly, it was based on the election of BC's real-life former coroner, Larry Campbell, to the mayoralty, a change reflected in the eventual change of title to *DaVinci's City Hall.*

Don Messer's Jubilee (CBC)

This musical variety series featured the talents of violinist Don Messer (1909–73) and ran from 1957 to 1969. I confess I have never seen an episode, but any long-running CBC staple that isn't *The Beachcombers* is, in my book, cool, by the very virtue of not being *The Beachcombers*.

Hinterland Who's Who (various networks)

Each of these 60-second interstitial segments highlighted a different animal found in the wilds of Canada, all set to a calming narration preceded by a soothing flute theme. After running their course in the 1960s and '70s, the segments were revived in the early 2000s.

The Littlest Hobo (CTV)

Everyone forgets that there was an earlier series (1963–65) before the one that most people remember today (1979–85). Both followed the adventures of a German shepherd that nomadically passed through different communities, helping those in need. So firm is its place in our hearts that *Corner Gas* did a brilliant parody in an episode called "The Littlest Yarbo."

North of 60 (CBC)

This drama series explored the challenges and troubles of First Nations residents in a sparsely populated northern community. It ran from 1999 to 2005.

Polka Dot Door (TVOntario)

From 1971 to 1999, TVO ran this children's program that featured music, animal segments and the infamous "Polkaroo," a person inside a suit that looked sort of like a green, two-legged giraffe (or perhaps a kangaroo).

Seeing Things (CBC)

Was it a mystery? Was it a comedy? Was it a paranormal procedural? From 1981 to 1987, this hour-long show followed a newspaper reporter (played by Louis Delgrande) who solved mysteries using his psychic abilities. If you wonder what Toronto looked like in the '80s, this is a pleasant way to find out.

Trailer Park Boys (2001–07)

Chronicling the adventures of Julian, Ricky and Bubbles, three small-time criminals, *Trailer Park Boys* was a huge hit and spawned a 2009 feature film. Shot on video instead of film, the production was as low budget as the show's premise—the residents of a trailer park get in and out of scrapes as they attempt to get rich quick or drink trying.

The Wonderful Stories of Professor Kitzel (various networks)

Though produced in the U.S., this series of animated history shorts featured many Canadian elements, not least of which was the voice of Paul Soles who famously also voiced *The Amazing Spider Man* from 1967 to 1970.

Yvon of the Yukon (1999–2005)

Airing on YTV, *Yvon of the Yukon* won multiple awards for its clever writing. The premise was this—an 18th-century French explorer named Yvon Ducharme is frozen in a block of ice. Three hundred years later, an Inuit boy named Tommy Tukyuk passes by with his dogsled team, and one of the dogs pees on Yvon's ice block, releasing him into the modern world. Hilarity ensues.

COOL CANLIT

Village of the Small Huts

Starting in 1982 and spread out over many different chapters, this ambitious and hugely popular play combined live actors, video and music to tell the history of Canada in fast-paced snippets that averaged about one scene per minute. Groundbreaking stuff for Canada in 1982.

Great Weeklies

If you live in a large Canadian city, the odds are that there's some sort of weekly tabloid-sized newspaper that deals with entertainment, pop culture and generally green, progressive, lefty-leaning, LGBT news and points of view with vaguely punk, alternative or pierced sensibility.

"The Maple Leaf Forever"

Composed by schoolmaster Alexander Muir to celebrate Canada's Confederation in 1867, the song solidified the maple leaf's already burgeoning reputation as a symbol of Canada. Purely as a point

COOL ARTS AND MEDIA

of interesting trivia, I should like to say that my great-grandmother was taught by Muir and, according to her, he was about as sympathetic a character as one would expect a 19th-century schoolmaster to be, which is to say, not very.

Cyberspace

Now largely fallen out of use, this term was all the rage in the 1990s to describe the conceptual environment in which online activity takes place. It was invented by ex-pat American (but now Canadian) science-fiction author William Gibson.

Guy Vanderhaeghe (b. 1951)

This two-time Governor General's Award winner is probably best known for his novels of 19th-century western Canada, *The Englishman's Boy* and *The Last Crossing*.

W.O. Mitchell (1914–98)

Mitchell's 1947 novel *Who Has Seen the Wind* was the archetypical "Canadian experience" novel.

Bill Casselman (b. 1942)

Casselman is the king of dictionaries and archives of cool Canadian words, sayings and slang. Thanks, Bill.

Yann Martel (b. 1963)

Martel is best known for the Booker Prize–winning 2002 novel *Life of Pi*, later made into an award-winning feature film.

Cory Doctorow (b. 1971)

As an ex-pat abroad, Doctorow is Canada's foremost proponent of intellectual property law that is neither evil nor stupid. As a writer of fiction, his best-known work to date is probably *Little Brother* (2007) for teens and young adults.

TOE TAPPERS AND STAGE STOMPERS

54•40

Since 1981, these Vancouver rockers have taken their name from U.S. president James Polk's infamous "Fifty-four forty or fight!" exhortation to encourage American expansionists to annex Canada. They were '90s alt-rock regulars.

Paul Brandt

Alberta's Paul Brandt (b. 1972) was working as pediatric registered nurse in 1996 when he struck gold with the song "My Heart Has a History," which rocketed him to international stardom.

Measha Brueggergosman

Probably Canada's most famous soprano, Brueggergosman (b. 1977) inspires almost rabid devotion from her fans and fascination on the part of the media.

Teenage Head

Formed in Hamilton, Ontario, in 1975, Teenage Head became Canada's most notorious punk band when a 1980 concert at the Ontario Place Forum turned into a riot. The forum banned music concerts for years afterward, and Teenage Head went on to further scandal-ridden success.

Terri Clark

Hailing from Medicine Hat via Montréal, Clark (b. 1968) is a country artist who has met with spectacular success both north and south of the border.

George Fox

In the late 1980s and early '90s, Fox (b. 1960) was the first of a new generation of homegrown country music stars. He continues to write and record music.

Glass Tiger

Formed in 1983 in exotic Newmarket, Ontario, Glass Tiger's most well-remembered hit is "Don't Forget Me (When I'm Gone)."

Honeymoon Suite

Having somewhat more longevity than other '80s bands such as Glass Tiger (see above), Honeymoon Suite was named for their hometown of Niagara Fall's reputation as the honeymoon capital of the world. "New Girl Now," "Burning in Love" and "Stay in the Light" are their best-known hits.

Colin James

Born in Regina, Saskatchewan, in 1964, Colin James is an award-winning blues-rock guitar virtuoso who has also enjoyed success in the neo-swing/big band genre. In 2005 he gave a command performance when Queen Elizabeth visited Regina.

Men Without Hats

Formed in 1977, Montréal's Men Without Hats is regarded by some as Canada's prototypical New Wave act, with its heavily electronicized hits, "Safety Dance" and "Pop Goes the World."

Nash the Slash

Arguably this nation's foremost performer on electric violin and electric mandolin, Toronto's Nash the Slash (b. 1948) also wears surgical bandages and sunglasses that make him look like the Invisible Man. Coolness quotient complete.

Platinum Blonde

More '80s bands! Toronto's Platinum Blonde had hits with "Standing in the Dark," "It Doesn't Really Matter," "Not In Love" and "Crying Over You." Nowadays, the singer is a well-known club owner in Toronto, and whenever I see him, it's all I can do to not ask him if he's the guy from Honeymoon Suite.

FROM FAR AND WIDE

Ogham Stone

So called because its markings undoubtedly resemble the Ogham characters used by ancient Druids, the Ogham Stone in Newfoundland and Labrador is believed to be proof that voyageurs from the British Isles may have come to Canada as early as 1000 CE. Others suggest that Vikings, known to have landed at nearby L'Anse aux Meadows at about the same time, could have left the marks, while still others believe they may be Aboriginal in origin. We shall probably never know, but mulling the possibilities never gets old.

Voyageurs on the Nile

In 1884, famous British officer General Charles Gordon was besieged in Africa and surrounded by enemy forces who were understandably sick of the British coming in and trying to steal all the land. Another British officer, Field Marshal Garnet Wolseley, was sent to rescue him. Wolseley had previous experience with this sort of thing, having ably assisted the Canadian government in suppressing the Red River Resistance (in which the Métis rebelled since they were tired of the British trying to take all their land).

Impressed by the Iroquois and French Canadian boatmen he had seen paddling the rivers of Canada, Wolseley arranged for a volunteer force of 400 men (of whom it is almost certain none were French Canadian or Iroquois) to paddle his expeditionary force of 4000 soldiers up the Nile to rescue Gordon. The Canadians went about halfway up the Nile before Wolseley decided to strike out overland and sent the Canadians home. It had been a grand adventure. Unfortunately for Gordon, Wolseley arrived in Khartoum on January 28, 1885—two days after Gordon had been beheaded.

Camels

In Canada, the gold rush was not populated solely by grizzled, bearded prospectors and high-kicking dancehall girls—we also had camels. Two enterprising businessmen thought that camels would make ideal pack animals for the prospectors and merchants of the Caribou gold rush. And with that, 23 Bactrian camels were introduced into an environment to which they were breathtakingly unsuited. The sharp rocks cut their soft feet, and they terrified horses. Most of the camels' owners eventually released them into the wild, where they spectacularly failed to breed.

Pirates

It seems counterintuitive to imagine cutlass-wielding buccaneers prowling our fishy East Coast waters, but that is precisely what happened in the 17th century, when there was a plenitude of loot to be robbed from cargo ships and other watercraft. Shiver me timbers, eh?

Privateers

If most of Canada's pirates (see "Pirates") were Europeans operating in our waters, our privateers (who were licensed to pillage the ships of enemy nations during times war) were the first generation of Canadian-born maritime raiders, seizing loot from (predominantly) America ships for sale at auction.

Marguerite de la Rocque (1500s)

As a young woman, Marguerite accompanied her relative Jean-François Roberval by ship when he was appointed first lieutenant general of New France in 1542. By the time their ship arrived in the Gulf of St. Lawrence, Marguerite was pregnant, having either convinced a lover to stow away on the ship or taken up with some young man on the long voyage. Roberval put Marguerite, her paramour and a nurse ashore on Île des Demons, off the coast of Labrador. Marguerite soon gave birth, but the infant died, as did its father and the nurse. Marguerite survived for three years before being rescued and returning to France.

Laurier Meets Diefenbaker (1841–1919)

In 1915, then Prime Minister Wilfrid Laurier had just gotten off the train in Saskatoon when a newsboy hurried up to him and sold him a paper. Laurier, attempting to make pleasant small talk, was told by the newsboy, "I can't waste anymore time on you, Prime Minister. I must get about my work." The newsboy was 15-year-old John Diefenbaker (1895–1979), who would go on to be elected prime minister himself in 1957.

Vive le Québec Libre

In July 1967, French president Charles de Gaulle visited Montréal to attend Expo '67. At that time, the province was seeing the first flames of the fire that eventually became the Québec separatist movement. Speaking to a frenzied mob, at the end of a short speech, he slipped in the phrase, "Vive le Québec libre!" which means,

"Long live a free Québec." The resulting international uproar was immediate. Both in Canada and back home in France, de Gaulle was criticized for sticking his nose where it had no business being stuck. He cut his visit short and returned to France, apparently quite pleased with the furore he had created.

Richard III's DNA

In September 2012, archeologists digging in a parking lot in Leicester, England, found what they believed to be the bones of King Richard III. The skeleton's spine was curved, in keeping with the traditional view of Richard as hunchback with one shoulder higher than the other. In their search for proof of the skeleton's identity, DNA researchers located a Canadian living in Britain, Michael Ibsen, who was descended from Richard III's sister. A comparison of Ibsen's DNA with the DNA extracted from the skeleton showed a match. In February 2013, it was announced that the bones of King Richard III had been found—with a little help from a Canadian.

WE WERE FIRST AT WHAT?

Canadians were first at many of things, most of them out-lined elsewhere in this book. The entries that follow are the spare ball bearings rolling around at the bottom of the casing.

Self-serve Grocery Shopping

The same way that Timothy Eaton pioneered the notion of having a fixed price (no haggling) for goods, in 1919, Thomas Primale Loblaw opened his first grocery store and struck a first for Canada by allowing his customers to select their own groceries instead of asking for them at a counter. Seemingly, Loblaw simply lifted the idea from the "general store" model and applied it to food.

Chiropractic Medicine

Chiropractic medicine was invented by Daniel David Palme (1845–1913) who was born in Pickering, Ontario, and moved to the U.S. when he was 20. He developed the method of spinal manipulation that came to be known as chiropractic (not to be confused with chiropody, which is foot doctoring).

Charge-coupled Device (CCD)

The chip that gives us digital photography was co-invented by two AT&T Bell lab technicians, Canadian Willard Boyle (1924–2011) and American George Smith (b. 1930). Since its inception in 1969, this little device has changed the world, giving us everything from handheld digital cameras to improved astronomical tele-scopes (notably a CCD retrofit of the Hubble Space Telescope).

"Instant" Replay

Early live television broadcasts were rarely recorded—if you missed something while watching a live broadcast of a hockey game, you missed it, and that was that. But one Saturday night in 1955, a *Hockey Night in Canada* producer decided to film the TV monitor during a broadcast to capture parts of the game. Several minutes later, after the film had been developed, it was broadcast, and viewers were able to watch critical plays over again while the game itself was still in progress. Not in slow motion, though—the U.S. network ABC instituted the slow-motion replay in the early 1960s.

BRIGHT IDEAS

Arborite

This material is the thin covering that protects many a counter and bathroom vanity. The U.S. equivalent is Formica. Both are melamine laminates akin to brittle plastic. Arborite is cooler because it's Canadian.

Electric Light Bulb

It would be too much to say that Canadians invented the electric light bulb, but a pair of Canucks, Henry Woodward and Mathew Evans, did receive Canadian and U.S. patents for a filament-based electric lamp. They later sold their patents to Thomas Edison, who had already been working on a similar idea for quite some time.

Electric Stovetop Cooking

Canadian inventor Thomas Ahearn may very well have been the first person in the world to use electricity for cooking. Although an American inventor had filed a patent for an "electro-heater" to be used for heating "victuals" as early as 1859, the device was seemingly never fabricated. Ahearn filed a patent for an "electric oven" in 1892 and almost certainly used a prototype of this device to cook a meal for an Ottawa hotel later that year.

The Fox 40 Whistle

After he was booed by 18,000 fans when his whistle failed to sound after an infraction, Canadian basketball referee Ron Foxcroft invented a "pealess" whistle. The whistle lacked the little cork ball, or "pea," that helped to produce the characteristic warbling whistle. The Fox 40 Whistle fast became a worldwide standard in professional sports.

The Grizzly Suit

By his own estimate, Ontario researcher and inventor Troy Hurtubise spent seven years and $100,000 designing and building a suit of armour that can withstand an attack by an adult grizzly bear. Looking like a cross between a deep-sea diving suit and the armour of Iron Man, the suit is over 2 metres tall and weighs 66 kilograms.

If the video available online is to be believed, the armour seemingly allows Troy to emerge relatively unscathed from such trials as rolling down the Niagara Escarpment, being rammed by a pickup truck, bludgeoned by bikers wielding two-by-four planks and whacked repeatedly by a large tree trunk swung from ropes. Having perfected the suit to his liking, Hurtubise has now moved on to developing a suit to withstand the blast of improvised explosive devices (IEDs) in Iraq and Afghanistan.

COOL MODES OF TRANSPORT

The Seabus

Connecting downtown Vancouver to the North Shore across the Burrard Inlet, the Seabus is a convenient and pleasant mode of everyday ocean-going public transit.

Newfie Bullet

This cynical nickname for a former Newfoundland passenger-train route between St. John's and Port aux Basques came about because the train took 23 hours to complete the 883-kilometre journey, at an average speed of 38 kilometres per hour.

Via Rail

Since 1978, Via Rail has been Canada's passenger train service. For long hauls, it is definitely more expensive than taking a bus, but it is a faster, smoother ride, is far more comfortable and you can buy sandwiches and drinks. It also tends to travel along more scenic routes.

Bus Travel

No one, given any other option, *wants* to take a bus over any significant distance. But if you *must,* this slow, uncomfortable and uncivilized mode of transportation, when sat in for hours and hours, gives you a sense of the fortitude, stamina and courage the early explorers of Canada must have shown—and they didn't even *have* buses.

Bateaux

These smallish boats, often pointed at both ends, could be propelled by paddle, oars or sail, depending on their function. Ranging from just a couple of metres long to up to 17 metres, they were wide and flat-bottomed, perfect for hauling a load of furs up a shallow river. Sometimes also called "longboats," bateaux (French for "boats") played a key role in the development of Canada. Bill Johnston, the so-called "Pirate of the Thousand Islands," famously used a bateau to conduct his hit-and-run raids in the present-day Kingston-Ganonoque region.

Chestnut Canoes

From their inception in the late 19th century to the end of the company in 1979, Chestnut Canoes, based in Fredericton, Nova Scotia, made some of the finest wood and canvas canoes in the world. U.S. president Teddy Roosevelt famously purchased Chestnut canoes to outfit his 1913–14 South American expedition.

140 Kilometres of Straight Track

I wouldn't have thought that knowing which country has the longest stretch of straight railway track was the sort of thing that anyone on earth would care about, but I'd be wrong. As it turns out, it's Australia, with 468 kilometres of perfectly straight track along a portion of the Trans-Australian Railway. However, if you're impressed by this sort of thing, then you can't fail to also be impressed by the 140 kilometres of straight rails between Regina and Stoughton, Saskatchewan.

Streetcars in T Dot

If you're one of the people fascinated by the straight rail track item immediately above, you're going to love this one. Aside from San Francisco, Toronto is the only other city in North America to maintain an extensive streetcar system. All the rest of the major cities have converted to light rapid transit.

WHAT WERE THEY THINKING?

Go ahead and try to dig up a good scandal in Canada—it's tough. Almost none of them are about sex, our attitude being that it's a cold country and we do need to keep warm. Sadly, most of the scandals in Canada revolve around money and politics, which can generally be relied on to provide less salacious photos than scandals predicated solely on the possibility that someone has stuck something where they, perhaps, ought not have.

The King-Byng Affair

In 1925, William Lyon Mackenzie King's Liberals lost the general election to Arthur Meighen's Conservatives (Remember Arthur Meighen? Sure you do. C'mon, don't be shy. What's that? You've never heard of him? But he was prime minister from 1920 to 1921! Still not ringing any bells? Don't worry—you're part of the majority.)

Mackenzie King clung tenuously to power with the support of the Progressive Party, though the Liberals had far fewer seats than the Conservatives. When embarrassing details about a Liberal bribery scandal began to leak out, Mackenzie King went to Governor General Lord Byng of Vimy (which, I realize, sounds suspiciously like a brand of socially ambitious mineral water) and asked Byng to dissolve Parliament. A dissolution would lead to an election but would also spare the Liberals from having to resign or being forced out of office. For three days, Mackenzie King importuned Byng to agree to a dissolution, but Byng rightly refused, and Meighen's Conservatives were asked to form a government. Meighen governed for about three months before his government fell and the Liberals handily won the following election. See? Nothing says "sexy" like the words "constitutional crisis."

Joyce Davidson and the Queen

My memory of Joyce Davidson is that she had a noontime talk show on CTV that was of such staggering banality that it doesn't have a Wikipedia entry, though Joyce Davidson herself (finally) does. You can get a sense of how seriously CTV took the show when you consider that it was half an hour long and featured Davidson herself plus one guest. Furthermore, the show's time slot immediately preceded *The Flintstones* as lunchtime fodder for kids coming home from school (of whom I was one).

Imagine my shock when I discovered that Davidson had a career prior to this show that consisted of outraging Canadians when, in 1959 as a host of CBC's *Tabloid* public affairs programme, she opined that, "Like most Canadians, I am indifferent to the visit of the Queen." *Collective intake of breath!* Well, that sort of radical talk may be fine at the Ceeb, but, by God, it doesn't play in Moose Jaw, least of all in 1959. Davidson's career in Canada concluded in tatters and she moved to the U.S.

Airbus

No one has ever accused former prime minister Brian Mulroney of being honest, but that's about the only thing he *hasn't* been accused of. In the early 1990s, two aircraft manufacturers—Boeing and Airbus—were competing for a big contract to supply Canada with jets. The contract eventually went to Airbus.

By a staggering coincidence, Mulroney, then *prime minister of Canada,* was given and accepted $225,000 in cash in brown paper bags by representatives of Airbus. During a 2010 investigation, it was alleged that the money was for work that Mulroney *was going to do* (on an unrelated matter) but never did. One is tempted to ask, "How dumb do you think we are?" but then, we did elect Mulroney no less than three times, so that question would seem to answer itself.

Gerda Munsinger

Finally, a bit of sex, but nothing really that interesting. Gerda Munsinger was an East German good-time girl ("prostitute" is such a strong word), who in the late 1950s and early '60s was simultaneously sleeping with two different cabinet ministers in that great bastion of moral rectitude, the Diefenbaker government. She was deported in 1961, but it wasn't until 1966 that the story finally broke amid allegations of espionage. The Canadian government swore that Munsinger was dead, but then a reporter from the *Toronto Star* found her alive and well and living in Munich. She matter of factly confirmed the sex and blandly denied the espionage. Gerda Munsinger died in 1998.

Tuna-gate

Largely forgotten now, the Tainted Tuna Scandal broke in 1985. The question was this: Did Minister of Fisheries and Oceans John Fraser knowingly permit the sale of tinned tuna that inspectors said *might* have been tainted? And if he did, was Prime Minister Brian Mulroney aware of it? Well, no one ever got sick, so nobody really cares, which just goes to show you that yesterday's spoiled fish is today's trivia book.

Peter Pocklington (b. 1941)

Where to begin? Carving out his empire in Edmonton, businessman Pocklington has had so many brushes with scandal that any list can be partial at best. As owner of the Edmonton Oilers, he famously traded Wayne Gretzky to the Los Angeles Kings after realizing he could not afford to keep him. Pocklington was taken hostage in his own house by a deranged kidnapper in 1982, and both Pocklington and the kidnapper were later shot in the police rescue operation. Pocklington used scab labour to break a meat-packing-plant strike in 1986 and was surprised when the Alberta government reneged on a sweetheart deal to end the strike. He is also widely suspected of having his father's name engraved on the Stanley

Cup despite his father never being a player, a coach or an owner. Finally, his millions made, Pocklington moved to the U.S. in 1998.

Conrad Black (b. 1944)

Since he was famously expelled from Upper Canada College for selling stolen exam papers, Canada's least favourite son has never failed to turn up on the wrong side of a sleazy deal. Surrendering his Canadian citizenship to receive a British peerage (Lord Black of Crossharbour, don't you know), Black made no secret of wanting his citizenship back after he was convicted in a U.S. court of embezzlement. He was sentenced to six and a half years in prison, of which he served only three and a half.

As of early 2013, Black is purportedly going to host his own TV talk show. Heaven help us. One assumes that answers to questions will be provided to guests in advance—for a price.

OH, CANADA!

There's no good way to categorize these bits of cool, and besides, it's nice to get a little hit of random mixed in with your cool, which has the effect of making your cool all the more cool, not to mention random, which I see I've said already. Better to just cut to the chase.

Stubbies

If you're of a certain age, you remember drinking beer out of these squat, brown bottles. If you're of a lesser certain age, you remember watching your elder siblings drink out of them. Either way, these little bottles have wormed their way into Canadians' affections, possibly because the McKenzie brothers used them, but possibly also because they are synonymous with nostalgic memories of childhood (*seeing* stubbies, that is; not drinking out of them).

HBC Blankets

If you're like me, you may think they're just blankets. It wasn't until I was well into my 30s that I discovered that these scratchy white or off-white blankets with colourful stripes of green, red, yellow and black are actually a signature ware of the Hudson's Bay Company, and therefore, to some degree, emblematic of Canada.

The Rhinoceros Party

This now-defunct (1963–93) satirical political party provided a welcome respite from reality with such strange platform planks as suggesting that the entire national deficit be paid with a credit card, advocating the painting of a boundary line in international waters (so the fish would always know which side they were on) and, after a prolonged absence from the political scene, announcing that their time away had simply all been a dream. Confusingly, a new Rhino Party was formed in 2006, which besides having the same name and non-goals, is held to be a different legal entity.

The McKenzie Brothers Theme

Depending on your temperament, this little vocal line, "Coo loocoo coocoo coo coocoo. Coo loocoo coocoo coo coocoo," is either pleasantly or irritatingly seared into your psyche as the show theme of hosers extraordinaire, Bob and Doug McKenzie. The line may have been based on the flute music of another icon of Canadian interstitial programming—*Hinterland Who's Who*.

Time Signal

"The beginning of the long dash following 10 seconds of silence indicates…" This precursor to the National Research Council time signal has been heard on CBC Radio since November 5, 1939. The long dash, when it *finally* arrives, usually indicates 1:00 PM Eastern Standard Time (1:30 PM in Newfoundland). It is regarded by some as Canada's longest running and shortest radio programme.

Rows of Replanted Trees

You're driving through the country and you see perfectly uniform rows of very tall trees. What has happened? Do we farm trees now? Well, sort of. We replant, anyhow, which is both economically and environmentally pretty cool.

Blasted Rock

In parts of BC and Ontario, you may find yourself driving through highway caverns of craggy rock faces blasted by dynamite to make a path for the road. Terrain like this makes for a cool drive. The added bonus is that the long shafts drilled for sinking dynamite are usually still visible in the rock.

J Cloths

These blue, yellow, green and pink reusable cleaning cloths (helpful household hint: you can wash them for prolonged cloth life) are distinctly Canadian. First introduced in 1966, they are so ingrained in our culture that it's easy to forget they're an "only in Canada" product.

Sex in the Snow

Besides being the title of a 1998 book by Michael Adams (about what makes Canadians different), this phrase has now, to some degree, entered the vernacular as a way to imply that Canadians are tough and like to have sex—just like the libidinously hardy reputation Australians enjoy, except without the wimpy attitude to cold.

60 Strokes a Minute

Get your minds out of the gutter; we're talking about paddling. The fur trade (and subsequent economy of Canada) was built on the strength and toughness of the voyageurs, capable of paddling their massive canoes at 60 strokes a minute and sometimes faster.

L'Assomption Sashes

Voyageurs were inevitably depicted wearing these colourful sashes, either around their waists or draped piratically from one shoulder, down under the opposite arm and back again. Taking their name from the Québec town in which they were made, the sashes have become visual shorthand for the presumed *joie de vivre* of the voyageurs, Gallic lotharios of the fur trade that they must undoubtedly have been.

Depression Glass

Given away at gas stations and other retail outlets during the 1930s, Depression glass was any cup, jug or other vessel made out of colourful glass. It was a cheap form of customer loyalty reward and could literally brighten the days of hardship-weary patrons. The glass still pops up at flea markets and auctions. While not specific to Canada (most of the glass was made in the U.S.), it is always a pleasant find at flea markets and auctions.

Glass Insulators

Resembling futuristic glass jars (but being solid glass), these prolific objects once served atop telegraph (and then telephone) poles to insulate electrical connections from the elements. Although they were used throughout the U.S. as well, they still pop up all over Canada, either selling for $2 or $3 at flea markets or perched on disused poles, where they have sat for more than 100 years. If you're on a long train trip, sometimes it's fun to count the number of withered wooden poles still bearing these reminders of bygone technology.

Centennial Coins

Now largely out of circulation, special centennial coins were issued in 1967 for the 100th anniversary of Confederation. It was always cool to get them in change because the animals on them were so beautiful: the silver dollar had a Canada goose; the 50-cent piece, a howling wolf; the quarter, a bobcat; the dime, a mackerel; the nickel, a hare; and the penny, a pigeon. Alas, now the mint issues special coins just for the heck of it.

Centennial Projects

Special coinage wasn't the only thing to come out of the Centennial. There were also books, TV shows, movies, buildings and any number of other projects to celebrate Canada's 100th birthday. If you're ever walking through a park and see a big, shiny statue that looks as though it might have seemed futuristic in 1967, it's probably a Centennial project.

Go to Hull!

Besides being a punny version of "Go to Hell," saying this immediately marks you as a Canadian, further suggesting that you may have grown up in Ottawa, where the drinking age was higher than the 18-year limit across the river in Hull, Québec.

Question Period

Whether you watch snippets of Question Period on TV or in person at the House of Commons in Ottawa, it's still time out of your life that you won't get back. Most Canadians view this block of time when MPs can hurl insults at one another (as opposed to governing) with affectionate loathing. If you go in person, you realize that hardly any MPs attend Question Period, and that those who do attend, sit in a cluster for the TV cameras, so it will look like they bothered to show up.

Barristers' Wigs

In Canada, our lawyers wear wigs and robes, just like in England. While it seems stuffy and anachronistic, it's still pretty cool.

Dick Assman

This gas-station owner from Saskatchewan was rocketed to fame in the mid-1990s after David Letterman kindly but firmly mocked his name on national television. The resulting bout of "Assmania" saw Assman appearing on the Letterman show for about a month. He pronounces his last name to rhyme with "Aspen."

The Maple Leaf (or L'Unifolie)

In other words, our flag. Not that most Canadians are flag wavers, but we have a pretty cool flag. Our nation is probably also the only industrialized country in history not to get our own flag until 98 years after we became our own country. That's in 1965 for those of you who aren't counting.

The Last Spike

I'm not talking about the spike driven upon the completion of the Canadian Pacific Railway in 1885, nor the book of the same name written by Pierre Berton about the building of the CPR, but rather a railway spike that had been spray-painted gold before sitting on my parents' mantel piece for years, having come as a promotional give-away with their copy of Berton's book.

Santa Claus

Living as he does at the North Pole, Santa is necessarily a Canadian. After all, according to Canada Post, his postal code is HOH OHO, so it must be true. How cool is that? Santa is one of us! I wonder if he drinks beer out of stubbies, complains about taxes and cordially despises Justin Bieber.

Bilingual Product Labels

If you've ever found yourself abroad turning over food packaging, looking for something you can't quite put your finger on and not finding it, but then realizing you expect to see French somewhere on the label, it's a good sign that you could be a Canadian.

"Canada 6, Russia 5"

At the height of the 1972 Canada-Russia hockey summit, all eyes (and ears) were trained on Moscow as the Canucks and the Russkies battled out the tie-breaking game. And at the Stratford Shakespearean Festival in Ontario, actor William Hutt plunged gamely onward, performing as King Lear to an audience whose attention he could sense was elsewhere. When he got word that Paul Henderson had scored his famous goal, he played out the scene, turned to the audience and said quietly, "Canada 6, Russia 5." He probably got a standing ovation.

"Just Watch Me"

Prime Minister Pierre Trudeau uttered these words in 1970 when asked by a reporter how far he would go to keep the peace during the FLQ Crisis (shortly afterward, Trudeau imposed martial law). These three words have entered the Canadian lexicon as either a symbol of arrogance or an expression of defiant confidence. The choice is yours.

Bren Gun Girl

Canada's answer to Rosie the Riveter, the Bren Gun Girl was a real person, Veronica Foster, who shot to fame during World War II when she was photographed rather sultrily blowing smoke on a machine gun at the John Inglis Company, where she worked assembling Bren light machine guns. She became the subject of an upbeat series of propaganda posters for the war.

"A Nice Light Snack"

This 1980s ad slogan for the distinctly Canadian chocolate bar Coffee Crisp entered the vernacular for years afterward, spawning an early millennial TV commercial in a which a father said it repeatedly to his children, who had no idea what he was talking about.

"When You Eat Your Smarties, Do You Eat the Red Ones Last?"

This Canadian ad campaign for Smarties candies went truly viral 25 years before anyone started using dumb-ass words like "viral" in contexts other than medicine. The ad featured catchy, quickly spoken lyrics set to a memorable tune, in which all the possible ways of eating your Smarties were systematically outlined.

COOL DAYS

*The special days that follow are either uniquely Canadian
in their character—or we invented them.*

Moving Day

In Québec, July 1 is known as Moving Day since many renters'
leases expire on June 30. Once legally binding, this now com-
monly observed tradition stems from the days of the seigneurial
system when the law was put in place to ensure that tenant farmers could not be evicted from their plots before the winter snow
had melted. Originally May 1 in the 20th century, Moving Day
was changed to July 1 so that students would not be forced to
move before the end of the school year.

Labour Day

The holiday that officially marks the end of summer is celebrated
on the first Monday in September, and then we all head back to
school (sigh). But did you know that Labour Day was invented in
Canada? On April 15, 1872, the Toronto Trades Assembly organized a parade in Toronto, and the Ottawa chapter followed up
with their own parade in September. In 1882, a 10th-anniversary
march was held in Toronto, and some visiting American union
reps carried the tradition south.

May 24

Also called Victoria Day (since it is Queen Victoria's birthday),
May 24 is now often referred to as May Two-Four, because it is
presumed that significant, if not heavy, alcohol consumption will
occur, with said boozing being metaphorically represented by
a case of 24 bottles or tins of beer, which in Canada is also known
as a "two-four."

Canadian Thanksgiving

In much the same way that Canadians are proud of their "funny money," by virtue of it being different than the American version, so, too, do we feel a patriotic attachment to our culturally distinct Thanksgiving, which falls on the second Monday in October.

La Fete Nationale du Québec

This statutory holiday in Québec falls on June 24—St. Jean Baptiste Day. Originally celebrated simply to mark the feast day of St. John the Baptist, the holiday slowly morphed into an expression of patriotic fervour and, since the mid-20th century, into one of Québec nationalism.

OLD AS THE HILLS

Scenic Caves

Located in Collingwood, Ontario, the scenic caves are wonders of nature that are cool to explore. Believed by First Nations to be mystical sites of spiritual uplift, the caves can indeed be places of magic and wonder. There's also zip-lining, a maze, a sugar bush (maple syrup) and a play area for kiddies not yet ready for vision quests.

Pier 21

In many ways Canada's equivalent of the U.S.'s famous Ellis Island, Halifax's Pier 21 was the gateway to the New World for thousands of immigrants coming to Canada between 1928 and 1971 to seek new lives or escape the ravages of war. The sprawling museum and interpretive centre (housed in the building itself) offer moving stories of lives long forgotten.

Wanuskewin National Heritage Site

Saskatchewan's 6000-year-old Northern Plains indigenous site is much more than an archaeological wonder. Visitors can walk down hunting paths twice as old as the pyramids and learn about beliefs and traditions that far pre-date European contact.

St. John's

Besides being the oldest occupied settlement in North America, St. John's, Newfoundland, also, according to some sources, has the highest concentration of bars in the world. If either of these facts seems incorrect to you, best to settle it over a pint.

Sucrerie de la Montagne

In the rustic hills of Québec, this small cluster of buildings cele-brates everything maple. If you like maple syrup (and really, who doesn't?), then going to a charming facility entirely dedicated to its production and consumption is not to be missed. You can see how maple syrup has been made for hundreds of years and dine in a 500-seat restaurant that serves traditional French Canadian dishes accompanied by equally traditional minstrelsy.

COOL HANDS-ON SCIENCE

Signal Hill

Signal Hill in St. John's, Newfoundland and Labrador, packs all kinds of cool into one location. In Canada's earliest days, it was used as a vantage point from which to signal with flags to ships at sea. The fortification-like Cabot Tower was constructed in the late 19th century to celebrate the 400th anniversary of John Cabot's voyage. And on December 12, 1901, it was the site where Guglielmo Marconi received the first transatlantic radio signal.

Ontario Science Centre

Set against the beautiful backdrop of Ernest Thompson Seton Park in Toronto, the Science Centre is a sprawling complex of hands-on science activities and exhibits. From lasers to frozen shadows to crazily tilting rooms, science comes amazingly alive.

Centre des Sciences de Montréal

You can save humanity in the interactive game Mission Gala, explore the human brain or check out an IMAX presentation at the adjoining Telus Theatre. There's more of course.

Science World

From toddlers to kids to teens to adults, there's something for everyone in this Vancouver centre. Exhibits let you do experiments to discover unexpectedly cool stuff about the human body, earth, wind and fire, as well as the world in which we live.

IT WAS WORTH A TRY

It's an old adage that we learn more from our failures than our successes. If that's the case, Canada must be one of the wisest nations on earth, not necessarily for the number of our failures, but rather for the sheer scope, ambition and stupidity of these memorable lapses in judgment.

The Selkirk Colonies

Thomas Douglas, 5th Earl of Selkirk (1771–1820), tried three times to colonize parts of Canada with Scottish settlers. His colonies in PEI (1803), Ontario (1804) and, worst of all, Manitoba (1812), all failed miserably. In PEI and Ontario, many colonists starved to death or succumbed to disease largely because of Selkirk's staggering incompetence in choosing settlement sites (for example, if you know that a particular plot of land floods every year or is already inhabited by First Nations treaty holders, it may not be a good place to set up a colony). In Manitoba, Selkirk's arrogance and stupidity directly led to the Battle of Seven Oaks (1816), which helped to galvanize the Métis as a political and military entity as they fought Selkirk's land-grabbing ways.

The MacAdam Shield Shovel

In 1913, on the eve of World War I, Sir Samuel Hughes (1853–1921), Canada's Minister for Militia and Defence, patented what would soon be known as the Macadam Shield Shovel (based on a suggestion from his secretary Ena MacAdam). The idea was to give Canadian infantrymen an entrenching shovel that could also serve as a small shield with which to deflect enemy fire. With the outbreak of war, Hughes saw to it that the Canadian army placed an order for 25,000 shield shovels. Unfortunately, the shield shovels were made from steel that was brittle and couldn't deflect a shot from a small handgun. It was also useless as a shovel because of a *hole* in the blade measuring 5 centimetres by 9 centimetres. The hole was for a rifle to be aimed through as the infantrymen cowered behind their protective shields…or *shovels,* whichever you prefer. The shovels were all scrapped at great financial loss, and Hughes went on supplying the Canadian military with useless weapons and equipment such as Ross rifles (that jammed) and Colt machine guns (that were considered obsolete).

R.B. Bennet Fails to Connect

When he defeated William Lyon Mackenzie King to become prime minister in 1930, R.B. Bennet (1870–1947) was in the unenviable position of governing a country in the early years of the Great Depression. Not that any one politician could have ended a worldwide economic downturn, but Bennet failed spectacularly to look as though he was even trying.

After a few rather half-hearted measures failed, Bennet defaulted to the Conservative ideology of the day—*laissez faire,* or "If we don't do anything, it will all just go away eventually." So reviled was he that when farmers who couldn't afford fuel had their horses pull their motor cars, these new conveyances were known as "Bennet Buggies." William Lyon Mackenzie King roundly defeated Bennet in the 1935 federal election.

CBC Cancels Regional TV News

For an entity created in part to foster a sense of national unity, you'd think the CBC would know better. In 2000, responding to a recent spate of heavy budget cuts, the CBC cancelled its regional supper-time news broadcasts. The "Corpse" (as it is called in some places) lost 200,000 viewers. and in many of the affected regions, viewership fell by 50 percent.

National Energy Program

Starting in 1980, Pierre Trudeau's plan to pay oil-producing provinces (mainly Alberta) a lower than market value price for oil in order to provide cheap oil to eastern provinces went over like the proverbial lead balloon. When you think about it, the idea was more like a lead zeppelin—crashing, burning and causing several casualties. The West was, seemingly forever, alienated from the rest of Canada and lost considerable potential revenue.

Long Gun Registry

It's difficult to say which aspects of the Long Gun Registry are the most regrettable—its implementation or the fallout from its eventual demise. Initially introduced as a sensible measure to help police keep track of rifles, shotguns and automatic weapons, the registry soon ran into trouble when the cost of administering the program ballooned rapidly and it was seen to unfairly penalize hunters in rural communities who had legitimate need for guns. Critics pointed out that, furthermore, criminals were the least likely to fall into step and register their weapons. But after years of debate, what surely counts as the biggest avoidable misstep was the decision of the Conservative government to merrily *destroy* the records of weapons that *had* been registered, giving a free ride to future murderers across the nation.

Scrapping the Avro Arrow

Already outlined elsewhere in this book, the Avro Arrow was an aircraft years ahead of its time. While it never went into full production, several prototypes produced in the mid-to-late 1950s were extraordinarily successful, but Prime Minister John Diefenbaker abruptly cancelled the program in 1958, pretty much putting Avro out of business with the stroke of a pen. Finally—surprise, surprise—all of the brilliant Canadian scientists and engineers who had worked on the Arrow packed up and went to work in the U.S., bankrupting Canadian aerospace design for a generation. Thanks a lot, Dief.

Privatizing Air Canada

It will be better for consumers, we were told. Competition will spur lower ticket prices and better customer service, we were told. It will be better for consumers, we were told again. Not! Sorry, folks, but the privatized Air Canada sucks. Everything about it sucks. Can we please put it back the way it was?

ATHLETE NICKNAMES

Little Chocolate (1870–1908)

At 5 feet 3½ inches tall, George Dixon was no giant, but his height didn't stop him from being the first-ever black world boxing champion. He also *invented* shadow boxing.

The Chicoutimi Cucumber (1887–1926)

The Montréal Canadiens' legendary goalie Georges Vezina got his nickname because he was from Chicoutimi and was calm under fire in the crease. From 1946 to 1982, the NHL's Vezina Trophy was awarded to the goaltender who let in the fewest goals. The Vezina Trophy is now awarded to the goalie judged to be the "best," while the Jennings Trophy is awarded for the fewest goals allowed during regular-season play.

Rocket Richard (1921–2000)

From 1942 to 1960, Maurice Richard was the Montréal Canadiens' not-so-secret weapon, becoming the first player to score 50 goals in 50 games and also the first to score 500 goals over the course of a career.

Canada's Sweetheart (1928–2012)

Barbara Ann Scott was an Olympic champion, world champion and Canadian national champion figure skater.

Grapes (b. 1934)

Known for his loud suits and louder mouth, sports commentator Don Cherry started life as a professional (albeit not very successful) hockey player and later coach. Now better known for his caustic and usually witless commentary on TV broadcasts of hockey games, Cherry's nickname "Grapes" gives you an idea of the mentality of his fans and supporters—cherries are small, round fruits and so are grapes, which means they're the same thing, so let's call Don Cherry "Grapes."

The Pod (b. 1957)

Steve Podborski was one of the infamous team of "Crazy Canucks," Canadian alpine skiers in the 1970s and '80s who achieved their remarkable speeds with what appeared to be a reckless style that invited disaster.

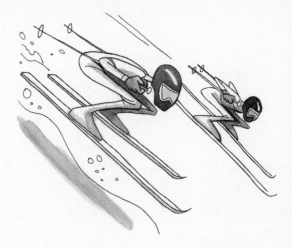

The Great One (b. 1961)

This is the familiar sobriquet of Canada's record-busting hockey player, Wayne Gretzky.

Schmirler the Curler (1963–2000)

Sandra Schmirler was a three-time world champion curler who tragically died from cancer at the age of 36. Near the end of her life, she bravely embarked on a new career as a TV commentator for curling events, cementing her moniker as a rare instance in which a person's nickname rhymes with the name of their sport. Today, the Sandra Schmirler Foundation raises money for newborns in medical crisis.

NO NICKNAMES, STILL COOL

- **Tom Longboat (1887–1949):** Champion long-distance runner from the Brantford First Nation.

- **George Chuvalo (b. 1937):** Professional heavyweight boxer, never knocked off his feet in 93 professional fights. Fought most of the other great boxers of his day. To say he "went the distance" is an understatement.

- **Nancy Green (b. 1943):** Champion skier (many times over), Olympic gold medallist, voted Canada's athlete of the 20th century, Conservative senator.

- **Toller Cranston (b. 1949):** Champion figure skater. Painter. Author.

- **Ken Read (b. 1955):** Champion alpine skier. One of the Crazy Canucks.

- **Silken Laumann (b. 1964):** Olympic multi-medallist in rowing.

- **Lennox Lewis (b. 1965):** Olympic gold medallist in boxing.

- **Donovan Bailey (b. 1967):** Record breaker and Olympic gold medallist in the 100 metres. For a time, the world's fastest man.

- **Elvis Stojko (b. 1972):** Figure skater with Olympic medals and championships coming out the ying yang.

- **Cindy Klassen (b. 1979):** Olympic multi-medallist in long-track speed skating.

MONSTERS

It's a bird! It's a plane! Hey, no, seriously, what is that? Well, it could by a mysterious, upright figure stomping through the woods and leaving giant footprints or strange, wave-like coils rolling across the surface of a lake or perhaps it's an erratically moving light on the horizon. You could always ask the family that lives next door, but they went to the store for maple syrup last week and no one has seen them since.

Bigfoot

Out of the corners of eyes all across the land, this towering, bipedal, hairy hominid has been a sometime fixture of Canadian cryptozoology since before the arrival of the Europeans.

Ogopogo, Manipogo and Igopogo

These serpent-like cryptids are said to occupy Lake Okanagan, Lake Manitoba and Lake Simcoe, respectively. Sadly, in recent years, Igopogo has been renamed "Kempenfelt Kelly." The same folks are trying to rename Bigfoot, "Pacific Pattie."

Other Sea Serpents

Not to be outdone, plenty of other Canadian lakes are said to have wriggly creatures lurking in their depths: Memphre in Québec's Lac Memphremagog, Old Ned in New Brunswick's Lake Utopia and Cressie in Newfoundland's Cressie Lake.

Old Yellow Top

Also known as "Precambrian Shield Man," this seldom-seen creature is described as walking upright, with its head often having yellowy blond hair or fur. Old Yellow Top has been sighted a handful of times over the last 100 years near Cobalt, Ontario.

The Pembroke Wildman

In August 1883, a small island in the Ottawa River hosted two sightings of a hairy beast that was eight feet (2.4 metres) tall and apparently had a foul temper. Shaped like a human but covered in thick, black hair (and according to one witness, also dressed in knickerbocker pants and a vest), the strange creature frightened off a family of campers and later menaced two "monster hunters" with a cudgel and a tomahawk. It seems the wildman flung the tomahawk at the hunters as they fled in their boat and broke one of the men's arms.

Windigo

An invasive spirit in the Algonquian tradition, the Windigo is said to turn humans into vicious cannibals. As you might well imagine, in a history as long and as hungry as Canada's, there have been more than a few Windigo incidents. Windigos can also appear in the form of much scarier and more aggressive Bigfoot-like creatures.

Turtle Lake Monster

Could it be a giant turtle, you ask? No, it's a Loch Ness–style plesiosaur sort of creature that boaters on Saskatchewan's Turtle Lake report seeing once or twice a year.

UFO GREATEST HITS

Falcon Lake, MB (1967)

One of Canada's most famous UFO encounters saw rock hunter Stephen Michalak encounter two low-hovering, saucer-shaped crafts that left a grid-like burn on his stomach, singed the ground and unusually high radiation readings at the landing site.

Langenburg (1974)

In 1974, Saskatchewan canola farmer Edwin Fuhr encountered four spinning discs as he was swathing his crop. They leapt into the sky, and he never saw them again. However, the site was still radioactive when tested 30 years later in 2004.

Dr. David Gottlib

In the midst of the UFO-mania of the mid-1990s, Toronto psychotherapist Dave Gottlib offered a solitary voice of clinical sanity. He noted that when people who reported traumatic UFO abduction experiences were treated by trained professionals instead of self-trained hypnotists known as UFO "investigators," the upsetting abduction experiences seemed to greatly diminish and in some cases went away altogether.

The UFO Report

Each year, writer and UFO researcher Chris Rutkowski assembles and publishes (online or in print) a comprehensive round-up of UFO experiences from across Canada.

Invasion Over Ottawa

On the evening of February 14, 1914, Ottawa, like the rest of the country, was ill at ease because Canada had entered World War I a few months earlier. When mysterious lights appeared overhead, the city (at a time when *any* aircraft were still a novelty), the powers that be thought it was a very real possibility that enemy saboteurs had entered Canadian airspace. Lights all over the city were doused, and snipers were positioned on rooftops. In reality, some jackass pranksters from upstate New York had set adrift paper balloons heated by candles to give them lift. These merry jokesters had been celebrating the 100th anniversary of the end of the War of 1812. The U.S., not having yet entered World War I, didn't seem to be aware that Canada was a nation at war.

Carp (1989–present)

Having appeared on the U.S. TV show *Unsolved Mysteries*, this incident in Carp, Ontario, is already well documented. It centres around an incredibly grainy VHS tape with some flashing lights on it and a broad cast of characters about half of whom appear to be reasonable skeptics, while the other half come across as incompetent, mendacious and possibly irrational opportunists.

Shag Harbour

In 1967, after observing strange blinking lights, numerous witnesses in Nova Scotia—including RCMP officers and a pilot—saw a bright flash and heard a big explosion as a large object seemed to crash into the ocean. A search turned up some strange, sulphurous, yellow glowing foam that almost immediately evaporated. No other wreckage has ever been found, nor any explanation offered.

Shirley's Bay

Canada's first (and as far as we know, only) government-sanctioned UFO spotting station was set up at Shirley's Bay, Ontario, in the early 1950s. The station's one and only even moderately close(-ish) encounter came when it detected a massive electromagnetic anomaly in the skies, which, wouldn't you know it, was obscured that day by heavy cloud cover and fog.

LEGENDS

Ghost Ships

From the East Coast to the West and in between, Canada has fielded more than a few ghost ships, apparitions of ships long since sunk. Mahone Bay, Nova Scotia, is the spectral home of the ghost of an American privateer, *Young Teazer,* set afire during the War of 1812. Boaters in the Northumberland Strait have been reporting sightings of a burning three-masted schooner since 1876 (long enough for any earthly fire to have burnt itself out). In BC, a ghostly echo of the *Valencia* (sunk in 1906) spookily prowls coastal waters. And the Great Lakes have a tradition of ghost ships, which are covered amply in books far longer than this one.

Loup Garou

The *loup garou* is the Québec version of a werewolf. These tales, often handed down orally from one generation to the next, might involve a sympathetic friend who was known to turn into a deer-devouring wolf during a full moon. Sometimes the donning of a special belt or other garment made of wolf's fur would bring on "the change," during which sheep and cattle would be killed and partially eaten. Notable to many of the stories is the likeable and sometimes innocent disposition of the person who turns into the *loup garou.*

The Money Pit

For more than 200 years, treasure hunters have been sinking vast amounts of money and resources into this little island in Nova Scotia's Mahone Bay. The cool (and slightly sad) thing about this legend is that even now that the site has been excavated with modern equipment to breadths and depths that would have been impossible in the late 18th century, the complete and utter lack of a single shred of reliable evidence that anything valuable is, or ever was, buried there does not deter people from continuing to hope.

The Headless Sea Captain

Far predating Washington Irving's 1819 story, "The Legend of Sleepy Hollow," the headless sea captain of St. John's, Newfoundland, was first spotted in 1745 and has reportedly been seen many times in the intervening centuries, usually haunting his apparent home of Queen's Road.

The Headless Nun

Sea captains weren't the only East Coast notables losing their heads in the 18th century. Sister Marie Inconnus (*sans* noggin) has been haunting Fort French Cove, New Brunswick, ever since she was nastily decapitated by brigands who may have been seeking to learn the whereabouts of a large cache of money that Sister Marie oversaw to supply an Acadian refugee.

MYSTERIOUSLY COOL

Not everyone in this section is necessarily a criminal, but where there is mystery, uncertainty and/or genius outrageous in its scale and ambition, there is a reprehensible sort of coolness, notable for being unexpected and surprising if not always pleasant, admirable or legal.

Gerald Vincent Bull (1928–90)

Accounts of Bull's life story read like the résumé of a James Bond villain. A brilliant scientist frustrated by the lack of support in his native Canada agrees to build a "super gun" for the Iraqi government. At 150 metres long and with a one-metre bore, it is to be used for launching satellites into orbit (seriously), but many worry that Iraq is really after Bull's expertise in missiles. Before he can complete work on either project, Bull is assassinated by a person or persons unknown in 1990.

The Mad Trapper (d. 1932)

Despite modern DNA testing, we still have no idea of this man's true identity. Under the pseudonym of "Albert Johnson," this reclusive hunter, trapper and probably poacher first survived the RCMP dynamiting of his remote Yukon cabin by hiding in a foxhole he'd dug underneath it. Then he killed a Mountie and led the RCMP on a 240-kilometre foot chase that lasted for more than a month. Finally, the Mounties brought in famed bush pilot Wop May (see p. 231), who realized that Johnson was eluding his pursuers by walking in the tracks of caribou herds. Killed in a firefight, Johnson took the secret of his true identity and history with him to his grave.

Kenora Bomber (d. 1973)

As with the Mad Trapper (above), despite recent DNA testing, no one knows who this person was or what motivated him to take the actions he did. On May 10, 1973, an "elderly" man of about 50 walked into the Bank of Montreal in Kenora, Ontario, wearing a stocking over his face and six sticks of dynamite strapped to his chest. Held in his teeth was a "deadman's switch"—a clothespin wired to the explosives. If the robber's teeth relaxed, the ends of the clothespin would make contact and the bomb would detonate. The so-called Kenora Bomber was making his getaway with about $100,000 in cash and an undercover cop as a hostage, when he was felled by a police sniper's bullet. The bomb detonated, and all that was left of the bank robber was one of his hands.

Jerome (d. 1912)

One day in 1863, the residents of Digby Neck, Nova Scotia, noticed a strange ship tacking back and forth out at sea. They thought no more of it, but the next day, an eight-year-old boy strolling along the shore realized that what he had taken for a beached otter some distance ahead was a young man of about 19 whose legs had been amputated and the stumps carefully bandaged. He had a jug of water and some bread with him.

Once he was nursed back to health, he began to speak, but he did so sparingly. The most anyone ever got out of him was that he was from what sounded like "Trieste," and the ship that had marooned him was called the *Colombo*. His legs had possibly been injured by "chains" and then amputated on a table. Observers noted that he was generally silent and resigned as though he felt he was serving penance for some past transgression. Foreshadowing Canada's later adoption of universal health care, local Acadian families cared for Jerome until he died in 1912.

Gunpowder Gertie

In the late 1890s and early 1900s, the infamous female pirate Imogen Stubbs (a.k.a. Gunpowder Gertie) prowled the waters of BC's Kootenay River system on a steam-powered launch with a Gatling gun mounted to the deck. Her profitable reign of piracy ended with her arrest in 1903, and she subsequently died in prison. The cool thing about Gunpowder Gertie is that she never existed. Created by BC school teacher Carolyn McTaggart as way to capture her students' imaginations, Gertie went on to achieve a reality of her own, after appearing in local papers as an elaborate April Fool's Day joke and later being reported as real by the CBC Radio segment *This Day in History*. Once the confusion was cleared, Carolyn McTaggart decided to put her obvious talents to use as a teller of tales for kids. Memorably, Gunpowder Gertie's adopted family motto is *Illegitimus non Carborundum* ("Don't let the bastards grind you down").

Igor Gouzenko (1919–82)

This cipher clerk in the Russian Embassy in Ottawa almost single-handedly started the Cold War, when, one night in 1945, he left work with a briefcase stuffed with top-secret documents that would reveal the existence of a vast network of Soviet spies and double agents operating throughout North America. When he finally found someone who took his story seriously, the resulting scandal was explosive, and Gouzenko spent the rest of his life making media appearances wearing a pillowcase over his head to make identification difficult for any vengeful Russian assassins who might be after him. He also wrote a 1954 Governor General's Award–winning novel, *The Fall of a Titan*.

The Boyd Gang

Seen by some as Canada's John Dillinger, Edwin Alonzo Boyd led his gang of bank robbers on a high-profile robbery spree through Toronto's banks between 1949 and 1951 during which time they perpetrated a minimum of six robberies, possibly more. Once captured, Boyd and various gang members escaped from prison and went their separate ways. Although Boyd was not present, another gang member shot and killed police detective Edmund Tong. The escaped convicts were all recaptured, but they proceeded to escape for a *second* time, despite being the most infamous and (poorly)

COOL MYTHS, MYSTERIES AND WHAT IFS

guarded men in the country. A huge manhunt ensued, and the men were finally captured for good in 1952. The two gang members present at the murder of Detective Sergeant Tong were hanged. Boyd was given eight life sentences but was released in 1962 (life apparently not lasting as long as it once did). He changed his name and went to live in BC, dying there in 2002 at the age of 88, two weeks after confessing to the murder of a couple in Toronto's High Park in 1947.

Rocco Perri and Bessie Starkman

Hamilton's most famous 20th-century mobsters were unusual for being an equally matched husband and wife team. As wildly successful 1920s bootleggers, Rocco provided the charm, while Bessie was renowned for her business acumen. When Rocco had to spend six months in a "reformatory," Bessie took over completely and moved into the profitable new area of narcotics. She remained in charge once Rocco was released until she was murdered one night in 1930 as the drunk couple was returning home from a party. A broken man, Rocco struggled on until he disappeared without a trace in 1943.

Cassie Chadwick

Born Elizabeth Bigley in 1857, this wily Canadian fraudster embarked on a career of small-time fraud, passing bad cheques and living under a string of different aliases. She assumed her final pseudonym when she moved to the U.S. and married Cleveland doctor Leroy Chadwick after they met at a brothel she was running (though she claimed to be completely unaware that it was brothel, protesting instead that it was a respectable rooming house). Happily married, but without her husband's knowledge, she set about her most famous and lucrative scam. Between 1897 and 1904, she bilked between $10 and $20 *million* out of gullible dupes by implying that she was the illegitimate daughter of American tycoon Andrew Carnegie. She was caught and sent to jail where she died in prison on her 50th birthday in 1907.

Ambrose Small

One of Canada's most famous disappearances still has us guessing after more than 90 years. On December 2, 1919, wealthy Toronto theatre owners Ambrose Small and his wife, Theresa, finalized the sale of their theatre chain and pocketed a downpayment cheque for $1 million. After a victory lunch with their lawyer, Ambrose and Theresa made plans to have a celebratory supper that night, but she never saw him again. Although there is strong circumstantial evidence that Small was murdered by his theatre manager, James Doughty, Ambrose's body was never found.

Doughty was only ever tried for embezzlement, since at that time in Canada, to lay a charge of murder, there had to be a body as well as signs that a murder had been committed. Rumours that Theresa and Doughty were lovers are completely and utterly unsubstantiated.

NEVER A DULL MOMENT

Non-residents seem to define Canada by its weather, which means snow, snow and more snow. For Canadians, the weather is just weather, to be endured if it can't be cured (which it really can't). Some people have suggested that our nation's weather is what gives Canadians their resilient, stoic nature; after all, if you can weather a Canadian winter, the rest of life's (non-seasonal) ups and downs shouldn't really faze you.

Midnight Sun

True, you must be in the Arctic Circle to witness this phenomenon, but along with Mounties and igloos, another stereotypical way of looking at Canada is that it is the "land of the midnight sun." During the summer, the sun may not set for as long as two months in the Arctic, which is cool if you like sunlight, not so much if you have trouble falling asleep when it's still light out.

Don't Like the Weather? Just Wait Five Minutes

This little piece of advice is nowhere truer than in Vancouver, where it's possible to experience sunlight, clouds, rain and snow in the course of about 10 minutes. This means that for the weather to simply change once, it might take only two and a half minutes (not that we're counting). This sarcastic nugget of truth rings true for many parts of the rest of Canada, too.

Yoho Blow

In BC, strong winds sometimes whistle and roar down the Kicking Horse Valley in Yoho National Park. "Yoho," said to come from a Cree word describing "amazement," is the name locals give to these gales, and it comes across as both friendly and awe inspiring.

Alberta Clipper

Americans may use this term unfavourably when describing a biting, windy weather system that has moved in from north of the border. However, Albertans will use it with pride to describe cold, steady winds that can reach 100 kilometres per hour.

Weather in Atlantic Canada

The weather on the East Coast is sometimes very nice, but often cold, ferocious and wet, and it is not for the faint of heart. It is credited with shaping the characters of Maritimers and Newfoundlanders as seen by the rest of Canada, the perception being that the people are warm, welcoming and more than ready to help friends, neighbours or perfect strangers in dire circumstances.

Winter in Québec

Winter in Québec is cold, long and—highly celebrated! With fairs, carnivals and festivals held throughout the snowy months, winter in Québec exemplifies a typically Canadian response to adversity—throw a party!

Winter in Southern BC

If you really don't like winter at all, go to southern coastal BC, where Vancouver and Victoria have some of the warmest winters in the country. The weather can be warm and rainy, mind you, so if constant clouds and rain are not for you, you may want to live where it's cold and bright.

Northern Lights

Among the most beautiful and magical sights you can see in Canada, the northern lights are caused by solar winds skimming across the earth's atmosphere. While they are most easily seen in the far north, aurora borealis can sometimes also be seen in the Canada's southern regions, especially in the autumn. Northern lights may be a spectacular greenish yellow or may simply be beautiful sheets of dancing white light.

Satellite Tracking

Since most of Canada is not polluted by the light of cities, it's pretty easy to go somewhere dark enough to see tiny, luminous specks better known as satellites smoothly traversing the star-filled heavens. It may not be as exciting as a game of end-to-end hockey, but seeing your first satellite is an experience you'll never forget.

Names for Ice

Contrary to popular belief, the Inuit do not have 50 words for snow (see below), but in Atlantic Canada, there at least eight different ways to describe ice. "Ballicatter" is formed on the shore where waves crash at near-freezing temperatures. "Frazil" is slushy, half-frozen ice that forms in water. An "ice pan" is a broad sheet or chunk of floating ice. "Slob ice" is ice that is not fully frozen. "Silver ice" results when the wind has blown rain against trees or other objects to form a beautiful silver coating. "Slurry" is float-ing, slushy, half-formed ice that, not surprisingly, gives its name to the sweetened frozen treat/drink available in some variety stores. "Lolly" is floating slushy ice, largely the same as frazil, slob ice and slurry.

Inuit have more than 100 words for snow

I've included this entry as an example of an urban myth that would be cool if it were true, but it isn't cool because it's not true. Various Inuit dialects have different words for snow-related phe-nomena the same way that English speakers use the words "ava-lanche," "blizzard," "squall" and so forth. There are also suffixes that may be added to the root word for "snow" in a manner simi-lar to "snowstorm," "snow day," "snowsuit" and so on. But the Inuit do not have 100 different words for "snow."

The Saxby Gale

In 1868, a British naval lieutenant named Stephen Saxby predicted that a large, violent and destructive storm would hit Atlantic Canada on October 5, 1869. Amazingly, he was only off by one day, and on October 4, 1869, a massive hurricane struck the East Coast, causing widespread mayhem and destruction. The Saxby Gale is cool not only because of the unlikelihood of Saxby's pre-diction coming true in the time and place he specified, but also because "Saxby Gale" sounds completely cool to say, perhaps echoing the syllables of some fictitious secret agent, playboy and bon vivant: "The name's Gale. Saxby Gale."

Wreckhouse, Newfoundland

The region of Channel-Port aux Basques in Newfoundland is nicknamed "Wreckhouse" because the winds there have been known to reach more than 200 kilometres per hour, toppling people and houses and blowing trains off the tracks. According to local wisdom, it is the windiest place on earth after Antarctica.

FOLLOW YOUR SENSES

Scudding Cloud Shadows

Nothing beats going out for a walk or driving across the rugged countryside and seeing a cloud shadow racing across the ground like a wave front. Being a worldwide phenomenon, cloud shadows are not an exclusively Canadian phenomenon, but our nation's plenitude of open space makes them far easier to spot and enjoy.

Skating on the Rideau Canal

Skating in general is a beloved Canadian pastime in winter, but we have chosen to exemplify it by espousing the pleasures of skating on the Rideau Canal in Ottawa in particular. Skating at any time of day is delightful, but the bright sun of midday is especially life-affirming as the reds, oranges and purples of dusk are magical.

Cracking Ice on Puddles

Again, you can do this anywhere in the world where it's cold enough for puddles to freeze, but if you happen to be in Canada and are looking for a simple pleasure that is characteristic of long Canuck winters, this is definitely one of them. I'm 43 and I still do it.

Country Drives

Maybe it's because I'm just learning to drive now, at mid-life, but taking a drive in the country is nowhere easier or more pleasurable than in Canada. You can be smack dab in the middle of Toronto and hop in the car and see rolling farmers' fields in less than an hour (depending on traffic).

Rowing or Paddling

According to some sources, Canada has more than two million lakes. If not two million, the number of lakes in Canada is still a heck of a lot, so you might as well take advantage of these soothing, pleasant modes of water travel.

Horseback Riding

Riding a horse is cool, and we don't feel any need to provide proof of this statement since it's obviously true.

Riding a Bike

Aside from the massive commitment and physical effort, it's pretty easy to cycle across Canada, with the TransCanada Trail offering a reasonably smooth path where other roads fail and highways are simply too dangerous (or undesirable) to ride a bike.

SMELLS

Manure

Yes, believe it or not, some people like the smell of manure. The odour almost never fails to offend city slickers, but denizens of rural areas often breathe a sigh of relief at the first whiff when returning to the country after a time away.

Crisp Autumn Air

There's an indefinable smell to the cool weather of fall. The smell usually becomes noticeable when the sunlight turns its autumnal yellow and the evening shadows begin to lengthen.

Spring Thaw

The return of warm weather brings with it a rich profusion of smells: flowers, grass, blooming buds, shooting shoots and the indescribable yet pleasant scent of frozen mud thawing.

Skunk

Yes, it's an unpleasant smell, but plenty of people I know find the odour to be an oddly uplifting experience.

SOUNDS

Autumn Leaves Underfoot

Okay, it's not merely when you're crunching them under your feet that autumn leaves are cool, but also when you're kicking, dancing or shuffling your way through a deep gutter of them.

Canada Geese

The next time you hear a discordant honking that sounds vaguely like an airborne jalopy, look up and you'll probably see a flying V-formation of Canada geese passing overhead. Their distinctive out-of-tune "honking" is both reassuring and laughable all at once. Can national character be echoed in a bird whose voice is both funny and majestic? We would argue yes.

Foghorns

You'll have to travel to the West Coast, the East Coast or the Great Lakes to hear this sound. Ranging in pitch from the low burr we have come to expect to higher wails that sound like something out of *Star Wars*, foghorns have been lowing their plaintive warnings for decades.

Hockey Night in Canada Theme

Once hailed as Canada's second national anthem, the HNIC (a.k.a. "Hockey Fight in Canada") theme spent the majority of its life at the CBC but was then scooped by CTV when the rights lapsed in 2008. No matter where it's heard, this little snippet of music inspires a swell of excited anticipation in the hearts of hockey lovers all across the nation.

Loons

Having a prominent place in myths and legends, loons also keep a wingtip firmly in the real world, as evidenced by their unmistakably musical call, usually heard in late summer and early autumn. For many, the loon's song is a sadly beautiful echo of the immensity and solitude of Canada.

Mourning Doves

Looking like slim brown pigeons, the mourning dove's unique call can perhaps best be described as sounding like a slow, breathy loon for its front half, graduating to one chilly note, repeated three times for the back half of the call.

Red-winged Blackbirds

If you're close enough to hear their cheerily extruded warble, then you're probably close enough to their nest that they may want to dive-bomb you, which they probably will. Still, these are cool birds, just doing their part to protect their young and offering a heartening song while they do it.

"Remember to Bring Your Health Card"

No, it's not a cool sound of nature; it's the cool sound of free health care. Any Canadian who has ever made a doctor's appointment has heard some variant of this from the other end of the line just before hanging up. It's how you know you're in Canada.

Snow Beneath Your Skis (or Sled Runners)

Nothing beats a quiet winter, or spring day, either cross-country or downhill skiing (maybe dogsledding, too) and hearing the soothing hiss of snow under your skis or runners. There are other countries where people can do this, but for Canadians, these cool activities have connotations of a distinctly national character.

Stillness of a Snowy Afternoon

On certain winter afternoons, it seems you can *hear* the silence. Even in the heart of a great city, if you're in a wooded park, it's possible to experience a moment of true stillness where the only sound is the non-sound of distant air moving on its way.

SIGHTS

Autumn Colours

The changing colours of autumn leaves is not only a coolly colourful explosion of reds, oranges and yellows, but in some parts of the country, it's so spectacular that an entire seasonal tourist industry is built around this final vivid burst of photosynthesis on the wane. Just one more sight that makes country drives so delightful.

Evening Sun Reflecting off a Shorn Field

If you've ever been out for an early evening boat ride, you've seen how the sunlight reflects off the water in a single dazzling shaft that stretches to the horizon. And if you've ever driven across the Prairies in the fall at twilight, you've witnessed the beautiful trail of light shimmering off shorn fields, following the path between you and the setting sun.

Storm Clouds

Puffy popcorn thunderclouds. Heavy green rainclouds. Grey, wispy harbingers of snow. Watching storm clouds roll in is not fun if you've got some sort of outdoor venture riding on the weather, but aside from that, it's a humbling reminder of the extent to which weather has shaped Canada and its people.

Sunset in the Rockies

You'll have to be in the western half of the country for this one, mainly because that's the only place you can see the Rockies. The profoundly moving experience of watching the sun go down, preferably from the top of a mountain, is one you won't soon forget.

Sunrise Over the Ocean

With the profusion of islands on the West Coast and the abundance of ocean on the East Coast, you can witness this cool sight from

---

either end of the country. If there were a book of *Things to See in Canada Before You Die*, the sunrise over either ocean would definitely be in it.

Whitecaps

The little white crests of foaming water at a wave's peak can appear on roiling oceans or windblown lakes. Whether the water is a crisp blue or a menacingly deep green, white caps are a signal that a gale is blowing up out there and it might be a good day to stay in by the fire.

FOUR SEASONS

What better way to conclude a book about awesome Canadian things than by an appreciation of the simple seasonal delights that have shaped and continue to shape the lives of Canadians.

Autumn Afternoons

The yellow sunlight slants past the tree branches or through the window in a way that is both calming and exciting. Mellow fall afternoons are one of the reasons I'm glad I live in Canada.

Winter Days

Cold, yes. Snowy, hopefully. Whether they're bright-skied, slate-grey or squall-blown, winter days may be what has shaped our national character the most and for the best.

Spring Mornings

Spring mornings in Canada are the welcome hand-up after the pummelling of winter. The smell of mud mixed with the scent of fresh air readies us for the long days ahead.

Summer Nights

Whether you're in the city or far from it, summer nights in Canada are deep with possibility. Whether it's the chance of romance or the pull of the future, a summer evening is one of the things that makes this nation great.

ABOUT THE ILLUSTRATORS

Roger Garcia

Roger Garcia is a self-taught artist with some formal training who specializes in cartooning and illustration. He is an immigrant from El Salvador, and during the last few years, his work has been primarily cartoons and editorial illustrations in pen and ink. Recently, he has started painting once more. Focusing on simplifying the human form, he uses a bright minimal palette and as few elements as possible. His work can be seen in newspapers, magazines, promo material and on www.rogergarcia.ca.

Djordje Tordovic

Djordje is an artist/illustrator living in Toronto, Ontario. He first moved to the city to go to York University to study fine arts. He got a taste for illustrating while working as the illustrator for his college paper, *Mondo Magazine*. He has since worked on various projects and continues to perfect his craft. Aside from his artistic work, Djordje devotes his time volunteering at the Print and Drawing Centre at the Art Gallery of Ontario. When he is not doing that, he is out trotting the globe.

Roly Wood

Roly has worked in Toronto as a freelance illustrator and was also employed in the graphic design department of a landscape architecture firm. In 2004, he wrote and illustrated a historical comic book set in Lang Pioneer Village near Peterborough, Ontario. To see more of Roly's work, visit www.rolywood.com.

Pat Bidwell

Pat has always had a passion for drawing and art. Initially self-taught, Pat completed art studies in visual communication in 1986. Over the years, he has worked both locally and internationally as an illustrator/product designer and graphic designer, collecting many awards for excellence along the way. When not at the drawing board, Pat pursues other interests solo and/or with his wife, Lisa.

Patrick Hénaff

Born in France, Patrick Hénaff is mostly self-taught. He is a versatile artist who has explored a variety of media under many different influences. He now uses primarily pen and ink to draw, and then processes the images on computer. He is particularly interested in the narrative power of pictures and tries to use them as a way to tell stories.

Peter Tyler

Peter is a graduate of the Vancouver Film School's Visual Art and Design and Classical animation programs. Though his ultimate passion is in film-making, he is also intent on developing his draftsmanship and storytelling, with the aim of using those skills in future filmic misadventures.

Graham Johnson

Graham Johnson is an Edmonton-based illustrator and graphic designer. When he isn't drawing or designing, he... well...he's always drawing or designing! On the off-chance that you catch him not doing one of those things, he's probably cooking, playing tennis or poring over other illustrations.

ABOUT THE AUTHOR

photo: Cathy Ord

Geordie Telfer

GEORDIE TELFER IS A WRITER, occasional playwright and sometime performer who lives in Toronto, Ontario. During a checkered but happily misspent youth, he was the assistant director for the Toronto Studio Players Theatre School, a freelance set carpenter and, on one occasion, the reluctant wrangler of a monkey and a ferret. Currently, he writes mainly for web and sometimes for television, having penned several documentaries airing on Discovery Canada and Animal Planet. He fills most of his days creating content for interactive projects associated with Treehouse TV, TVOKids and for other children's broadcasters across Canada. He is also the author of five other non-fiction titles.